Dolphins

Their Natural History, Behavior and Unique Relationship with Human Beings

Galia Dor

Astrolog Publishing House

Language Consultant: Marion Duman

Cover Design: Na'ama Yaffe

Layout and Graphics: Daniel Akerman

Production Manager: Dan Gold

Drawings on pages 13, 19, 21, 25, 35, 61, 63, 64, 75, 87, 90, 92, 101, 118 - Galia Dor

The publisher and author wish to thank the *Dolphin Reef, Eilat, Israel* for the permission to use their photos.

Published by Astrolog Publishing House 2004

It is an important and popular fact that things are not always what they seem: For instance, on planet Earth Man has always assumed that he was more intelligent than Dolphins because he had achieved so much – the wheel, New York and wars and so on – while all the dolphins had ever done was muck about in the water having a good time. But conversely, the dolphins had always believed that they were far more intelligent than man – for precisely the same reasons.

Curiously enough, the dolphins had long known of the impending destruction of the planet Earth and had made many attempts to alert mankind to the danger, but most of their communications were misinterpreted as amusing attempts to punch footballs and whistle for tidbits, so they eventually gave up and left the Earth by their own means shortly before the Vogons arrived.

The last ever message was misinterpreted as a surprisingly sophisticated attempt to do a double-backward somersault through a loop while whistling the "Star Spangled Banner", but in fact the message was this: So long and thanks for all the fish.

Douglass Adams
The Hitchhiker's Guide to the Galaxy

White-sided Atlantic dolphins

Contents

Introduction

Our natural world is a fascinating, highly complex and still mysterious web, vibrating with millions and millions of interacting species that communicate and celebrate the diversity of life during each and every moment of their being. Among those dwelling in the waters of this world, one group has always fascinated the human mind both for its unique adaptation and intelligence and for its curious relationship with human beings. These are the marine mammals, namely, whales, dolphins and porpoises. This book, which concentrates solely on dolphins, aims to offer the reader a thorough, highly accessible work that encompasses everything that is known today about these curious animals and everything that is crucial to understanding them.

As a biologist, I have worked on and researched many different subjects, always seeking to study animals in their natural habitat and observe their behavior in the wild. I was very fortunate to be able to conduct observations of wild dolphins in the Red Sea and research the nocturnal behavior of dolphins in conditions of semi-captivity. Over and above the fascinating aspect of the research itself, I was able to communicate with them and be accepted as part of their world while swimming with them.

The first part of the book concentrates on the biology, evolution, adaptation, senses, intelligence and behavior of dolphins. It then goes on to deal with the alarming state of the global environment and its impact on dolphins in the wild in order to sum up their present condition and discuss some important issues such as tuna fishing nets, stranding, etc.

The second part of the book examines the mysterious question of the curious relationship between dolphins and humans: spontaneous swimming in the wild, cooperation between fishermen and dolphins, dolphins in captivity, training and therapy and the unique place dolphins have been accorded throughout history in literature, legends and myths.

With the hope of promoting the love, understanding and importance of these charming and graceful creatures, this book is dedicated to all the dolphins of the oceans, seas and rivers of this earth.

Chapter 1

Evolutionary adaptation to the sea

Dolphins are mammals. Perhaps this is one of the reasons for our fascination with them, since despite their biological resemblance to us, they nevertheless differ greatly in their external appearance, resembling fish and sharks more than the more familiar-looking land mammals. When we see a cow feeding her calf or a female cat defending and protecting her kittens, we recognize their "mammal-like" biology and behavior and do not need to be experts to recognize it. Thanks to a kind of biological kinship, we are able to identify with land mammals and their familiar characteristics – four limbs, mammary glands, maternal behavior, slow development of the young until they reach maturity, and sometimes soft, beautiful fur that just begs to be touched. This is one of the reasons why it is difficult for many of us to identify (i.e., in the sense of relating to a being entirely different than us) with insects, birds and reptiles. (Luckily, however, some people are fond of and interested in these animals precisely because they are so different and alien.) However, dolphins and whales are mammals like we are: they are warm-blooded; they use their lungs to breathe; they give birth to live young; the mother dolphin has milk-filled glands with which to feed her babies; and some of the dolphin species have very large brains in proportion to their body size, attesting to their high level of intelligence among other species (see Chapter 4 for further details.)

In addition to being different than land mammals, only a small percentage of people in the world have ever had a chance to watch free-ranging dolphins ploughing through the waves. This is no doubt another factor that enhances the 'mystic air' surrounding them.

Dolphins are fully aquatic and have been for the past 40 million years. This accounts for their anatomy, which reflects their superb adaptation to life in the sea. The evolution of the order cetacea (as we understand it today, even though many links are still missing) has its roots in land. In other words, this special group is believed to have evolved from furry land mammals called *mesonychids*. These ancient creatures, which wandered the earth some sixty million years ago, looked very much like the wolves of today, except that they had hooves like cows. It is a really tantalizing thought to imagine whales and dolphins evolving from such almost familiar land mammals. The theory that attempts to explain the evolutionary process that formed today's whales and dolphins considers those ancient mesonychids to be animals that spent their lives near swamps, lakes, estuaries and seas, trying to catch fish and various aquatic animals. As a result of spending so much time near the water and then partly in the water, their bodies began to change in an aquatic direction. Ten million years later, the first whale-like creatures evolved. These were archaeocetes, and while they resembled whales and dolphins, they were still much less adapted to the seas.

Alternatively, they did not spend all the time in the water, but returned to land – perhaps to reproduce (just like seals do). According to the theory, the archaeocetes vanished from the world around thirty million years ago, but at that time, marine mammals resembling the whales and dolphins of today were already spreading throughout the seas and oceans of the world. Modern species as we know them have existed on earth for a mere six million years.

The return of land mammals to the sea posed many difficult problems that had to be solved by the creative powers of evolution. Respiratory difficulties arose because in the three-dimensional world of air-breathing cetaceans, water pressures vary greatly and air is available only at the surface. Thermal problems occurred because the conductivity of heat in water is much higher than in air. There were also other issues that were crucial to their successful survival. If we first consider external features, a lot of changes have taken place since cetaceans returned to the oceans. This aquatic adaptation process, which lasted millions of years, "molded" dolphins and whales into their present shape. Generally, they have a smooth, streamlined, torpedo-shaped body surface with no apparent limbs (that is, legs and arms), but only side and back flippers, dorsal fins and external genitalia that are modified and well concealed under the skin. Again, this is not the familiar picture of a mammal that most people have. As evolution progressed, the body shape of dolphins and whales became closer and closer to that of other marine vertebrates (such as sharks). In contrast to land mammals, which are affected by the force of gravity, marine mammals spend their entire lives in the water, which frees them from gravitational limitations on their movements. Marine mammals are weightless in the water (hence the evolutionary viability of a huge creature such as the blue whale, which weighs 170 tons) and no longer require the limbs that support the body weight of land animals.

The limbs in marine mammals not only serve to control their movements in the water but also play a role in the physiological process of temperature regulation. The almost complete loss of the hind limbs (only the flukes remain) and the reduction in the size of the forelimbs (resulting in flippers) gave the marine mammals two important advantages: first, more efficient limbs for steering and controlling body movements; second, a decreased body surface, which is crucial to animals living in the water. It is important to remember that these are warm-blooded animals with a body temperature of 37 degrees Celsius, just like humans. This means that they need to maintain their body temperature in water at all times, which is more difficult than for land mammals because heat loss from the skin is much greater in water than in air at the same temperature. Thus, it is imperative for animals living in water – extremely cold water in some

species (the Antarctic Ocean, for instance) – to develop ways in which to cope with those conditions.

Another important parameter that must be taken into account is the rate of heat loss from the skin. This depends on the body surface of the animal. Body surface decreases in relation to the size and mass of the animal's body: as body volume increases, so body surface decreases proportionately. In other words, the bigger the animal, the smaller its body surface, and therefore, the lower its rate of heat loss. Thus, the great mass of the whales that inhabited polar waters played a crucial adaptive role, since it caused their rate of heat loss to decrease greatly. However, that is not the end of the body heat problems facing marine mammals. As opposed to land mammals, which have a broad range of behavioral tools for coping with cold and maintaining a constant body temperature (for example, growing thick fur, living in nests, curling up in caves and other protective places, huddling together, migrating to warmer areas, etc.), marine mammals have to rely mainly on a thick layer of fat, known as blubber, in their deep skin layers. The blubber serves as an insulator as well as a store of surplus energy. In fact, it is such a good insulator that it is liable to cause the diametrically opposite problem: overheating during increased physical activity. This problem was solved through the development of large arteries running through it and up to the skin. If a large amount of blood is pumped through these vessels, it warms the skin, which quickly dissipates the heat into the surrounding water.

Water also offers resistance to the forceful movements made by the animal's body or limbs. Researcher Peter Purves, who found the key to the dolphin's swimming pattern and speed, made a very interesting observation back in the 1960s. It seems that as the tail is moved upward by the dolphin's power stroke (a propulsive action), the water is forced down to the lower surface of the flukes, creating turbulence and a low-pressure area beneath the flukes. As the strokes continue, the blades of the flukes are drawn backward and this causes the dolphin to move forward and downward. As a result, the further upward movement of the flukes accelerates the passage of the water over the body and a strong thrust drives the body forward. The tail actually creates a "laminar flow" of water over the smooth body. The interesting phenomenon that caused researchers to examine the dolphin's ability to swim so fast was that according to calculations, in order for a dolphin to maintain its speed, the muscles of its tail would have to be ten times bigger and more powerful than its muscles actually are.

The smoothness of the dolphin's skin is not only the result of the lack of fur, hair or folds. There are special surface cells in its skin that contain oily droplets that lubricate the skin and enhance its unique smoothness.

Adaptation of the respiratory system

Dolphins dive into the water every few minutes and they sometimes dive quite deeply. Anyone who has attempted diving or taken a scuba-diving course knows that the human lungs and respiratory system are limited in their ability to withstand high pressure in deep waters. We need to be equipped with air tanks and follow specific and strict regulations in order to ensure that the pressure within our lungs is equal to or slightly higher than the pressure of the surrounding waters. In addition, the nitrogen in the compressed air dissolves into the bloodstream and is liable to penetrate the body's tissues. One of the most dangerous things a diver can do is to rise quickly to the surface of the water, because as he moves upward, the decrease in pressure causes the dissolved nitrogen to form bubbles. These bubbles can accumulate in the body and may invade the muscles as well. In divers' jargon, that condition is known as "the bends". If that happens, it is vital to evacuate the diver to an oxygen tank promptly as the condition poses an acute threat to his life. How did dolphins – and whales for that matter – solve this problem during their long process of evolutionary adaptation?

If dolphins dive to depths of over ten meters, their flexible chest area and lungs collapse in response. As a consequence, the alveoli – the pockets in the lungs where gases are exchanged with the bloodstream – are forced shut and the nitrogen-containing air is forced into the windpipe and bronchial passages. This is where the remarkable revolution happens: once the alveoli collapse, nitrogen can no longer pass into the bloodstream, and this is how dolphins avoid "getting the bends". Moreover, when dolphins dive to shallow depths of less than ten meters, their lungs do not collapse, but the nitrogen level in their tissues rises – a physiological situation with which they manage to live and cope. How? That is a question we not yet been able to answer. It has recently been discovered that dolphins may actually have to cope with the bends, and the manner in which they do so is currently being studied.

Anatomy

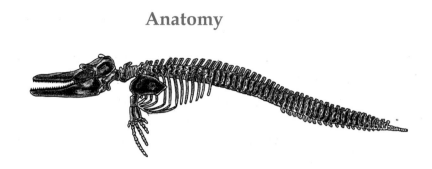

As we have just seen, the body structure of cetaceans manifests a remarkable adaptation to living in the water, but it also contains many characteristics that are indicative of their ancestors – land mammals – and are in fact common to all mammals in general. These are hair (e.g., vestigial hair – remnants of hair that is no longer "true" body hair); a four-chambered heart, a single lower jaw bone, three tiny bones inside the middle ear, mammary glands and a placenta, and are always found in both marine and land mammals. These are the signs that prove to us that in spite of their misleading fish-like appearance, dolphins are indeed mammals. The paddle-shaped flippers, which are the equivalent of human arms, help the dolphins steer and move through the water.

The structure of the head in cetaceans is one of the most helpful external features in recognizing species, but in general, most cetaceans have a prominent upper jaw that sometimes resembles a beak. The head carries a lot of weight in the form of the thick blubber that insulates dolphins from the cold water. Since this blubber prevents the major facial muscles from reaching the surface of the skin, dolphins are quite limited in their facial expressions (although some of them, particularly Bottlenose dolphins, are famous for their constant smile, which occurs for this very reason). The eyes of all cetaceans are small and quite expressionless. There are no eyelashes or eyebrows. The flippers vary in shape and size as well as in mobility and flexibility across the different species. Most cetaceans have rather similar features, but their skeletons vary greatly between species. The skull has departed from the normal mammalian structure by being "telescoped" (that is to say, compressed from front to back so that some parts overlap each other). The telescoping head in odontocetes (toothed whales) may be related to the structure of the melon – a lens-shaped structure in the dolphin's forehead that is associated with dolphins' echolocation ability. All dolphins have teeth, and these differ greatly between the species, but in general, they seem to have more teeth than land mammals (dozens of simple conical teeth on both sides of each jaw). The shape and number of teeth vary in accordance with feeding and diet patterns.

Where are dolphins along the evolutionary tree of life?

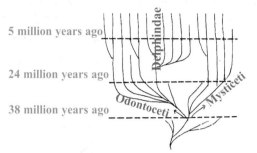

Dolphins belong to the order cetacea, but they are not alone in this group; the whales share place with them under this order. The order cetacea contains thirteen families and is divided into two sub-orders: the odontocetes or toothed whales and dolphins and the mysticetes or baleen whales. Baleen whales are generally much larger than toothed dolphins and whales. Instead of teeth, these whales have long, thin plates called baleen hanging from their upper jaws. These baleen plates are used to strain the huge amounts of seawater in their mouths and catch small prey.

The odontocetes include dolphins and porpoises, river dolphins, sperm whales and beaked whales.

The delphinidae or dolphin family contains over thirty species, ranging from the Chinese Yangtze River dolphin to the awesome killer whale – the Orca – which is actually a dolphin. The classification of the delphinidae family is rather confusing because it includes five whales in addition to dolphins. These are the short-finned whale, the long-finned whale, the false killer whale, the melon-headed whale and the pygmy killer whale. The distinct features that set them apart from dolphins are their large size, rounded heads, blunt beaks and fewer teeth. River dolphins are a fascinating part of the sub-order odontocetes, since they comprise a group of species that scientists and researchers worldwide are desperately trying to study. However, their small numbers, as well as their shyness and the current (unforgivable) polluted and devastated state of some of the rivers that form their habitat, are hampering the success of the research

It is worth mentioning that the division between toothed and baleen whales was questioned when the DNA of different whale species was compared at the beginning of the 1990s. The findings were surprising, since it turned out that the sperm whale (a toothed whale), for instance, is more closely related to baleen whales than to other toothed whales. It was later discovered that during the course of its evolution, the toothed whale was the baleen whale's ancestor. However, according to recent molecular discoveries

(Okada, 2001), there is a clear division between toothed whales (odontocetes) and baleen whales, which is parallel to the morphological and physiological distinctions between the two groups. The most likely ancestor of the cetaceans that belong to the present stage of evolution were mesonychids, which probably lived in lagoons in the tropics and were – significantly – carnivorous. However, baleen whales and toothed whales differ in their feeding strategies: the former filter-feed, while the latter hunt a single prey and employ extraordinary means such as echolocation to that end (see Chapter 2 for further details).

This difference might be indicative of certain changes in sea level or in the abundance of food that occurred – changes that led to different adaptation strategies for survival in the seas and the oceans of the world. According to Okada (2001), it seems that toothed marine mammals diverged along the evolutionary tree in the following order: sperm whales, Ganges River dolphins, beaked whales and then all the other freshwater and marine dolphins. It is important to remember, though, that the issue of the divergence of dolphins and whales is still fraught with controversy. The theory that river dolphins diverged at some point between sperm whales and beaked whales – both of which live in the open waters of the oceans, are deep divers and feed on squid – is quite problematic. Some still claim that sperm whales and beaked whales are more closely related to one another than to river dolphins.

Speaking of the environment in which dolphins live, we must keep in mind that their world is more dangerous than innocuous. Fearsome predators such as sharks, as well as the lack of places to hide in or swim to, presumably played a role in the development of a very high level of social and communicative skills. They had to rely on each other for protection, and it has in fact been recorded by observers in the wild that sharks opt to withdraw or at least do not attempt to approach a group of dolphins swimming together. In addition to the danger of predators, dolphins must sleep, reproduce and rear their young in an aquatic environment. Unlike fish, they do not simply release millions of eggs into the water in the hope that a certain percentage will survive, but must invest all their time and energy in the creation of one offspring. They not only have to nurse, feed and protect the small, relatively helpless infant, but they have to teach it the strategies and behaviors that are essential for its survival. Therefore, the task at hand is not an easy one and the various fascinating characteristics of dolphins, whether anatomical, physiological or behavioral, have developed as an evolutionary response to these special conditions.

**Photo: Galit Amiel. Dolphin Reef, Eilat, Israel.
Website: www.dolphinreef.co.il**

One very interesting characteristic of dolphins is the special way they perceive the environment and cope with it: their sensory world.

Chapter 2

The dolphins' sensory world

In addition to the obvious evolutionary need to alter physically – for example, the thick cushion of blubber to insulate them against the freezing cold waters in some regions of the world, the streamlined shape of their bodies, their hairless skin, the reorganization of the respiratory system with the blowhole located on top – dolphins had to adapt in other ways as well. Their sensory world had to change considerably.

Our sensory system is there to help us perceive the world around us and adapt our behavior accordingly. In a completely different world, dolphins "developed" ways with which to cope with their underwater existence. Without a doubt, the most fascinating of their unique senses is their ability to echolocate.

Echolocation

What is echolocation? It is the ability to produce intense, short, broadband pulses of ultrasonic sound that are bounced off different objects that happen to be in the dolphin's path. These sounds produce echoes that are heard by the mammal and from which it creates an acoustical picture of its surroundings. In fact, if you think about the ultrasound examination that pregnant women undergo, the picture perceived is pretty similar to what the dolphin might "see" using its echolocation sense. In experiments in captivity, it was shown and proved that bottlenose dolphins are able to find their way to a certain target easily even if they are blindfolded. The closer the dolphin gets to the target, the more rapid the clicks it emits. However, if you were to get close to a dolphin, you would find no apparent ears at all. In fact, the dolphin's external ears consist of nothing more than two holes located a couple of inches behind and below the eyes. The question that puzzled the scientists back in the 60s was how a dolphin, equipped with such small, almost non-existent auditory canals, could hear so well. To this day, scientists differ in their professional opinion as to how they do it (or 'how they manage it'). Most agree that the acoustic channel through which the sounds travel is the lower jaw. A few maintain that the auditory canals, though reduced, are still the main conduits to the inner ear.

However, we do know that the sounds are produced in a complex chamber in the dolphin's nose (which is located on top of its head). The sounds are then emitted in a narrow beam through the melon, a waxy, lens-shaped structure in the dolphin's forehead whose function is to focus the sounds. The returning echoes enter the inner ears through either the fatty tissues of the lower jaw or the auditory canals or perhaps both.

The inner ear of the dolphin is adapted to hearing ultrasonic frequencies far beyond the range of human hearing – well over 100 kHz. Dolphins learn about their surrounding simply via the time it takes the sounds to travel back to their ears. Moreover, dolphins can also learn about the size and even the material composition of objects since sounds differ in the way they bounce back according to different material densities.

Dolphins use this amazing tool in the detection and tracking of prey, either in individual hunting or in cooperative hunting with the whole group.

While echolocation is without a doubt a crucial tool in the lives of dolphins, it is not the only way in which cetaceans utilize sounds. The fact that they live in water is in itself an important element. Sounds travel much more effectively through water than through air. A dolphin living in the underwater world hears a very rich and perhaps even confusing cacophony of sounds – clicks, squeaks, groans and many other sounds that are produced by the vast and varied body of underwater creatures. We believe that the dolphin is capable of differentiating between these sounds and learning a great deal about the world around it simply by listening.

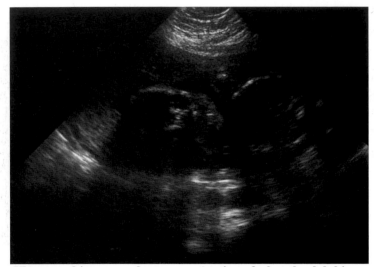

Ultrasound image: a close representation of what the dolphin might "see" using its echolocation sense.

Besides echolocation sounds, dolphins produce other communicative sounds as well, such as signature whistles, squeals, chirps and grunts – a highly complex system about which, despite intensive research, we still have rather limited knowledge. However, we are acquainted with one fascinating phenomenon. The acoustic world and ability of dolphins has evolved to such a degree that a dolphin can (and does) use echolocation while searching for food, at the same time using whistles to communicate with other dolphins. The fact that the frequency of echolocation sounds does not overlap the frequency of other sounds emitted by the same dolphin permits different sounds to be created simultaneously and enables signals emitted by other dolphins to be perceived and interpreted (see Chapter 5 for further details).

Some scientists from other fields are fascinated with the dolphins' sonar system since the creation of a similar device (much more sophisticated than ultrasound systems) would have numerous applications in everyday life and scientific endeavors. It could, for instance, pick up the fine details of any object. Some researchers are very interested in mimicking the beams sent by dolphins and hope to be able to put the technique into practical use one day. The problem is that while a computer can depict the sounds on a screen in many ways, according to their wave pattern and frequencies, the result resembles a complex tangle of strings to the human eye. A group in the Maryland Naval Surface Warfare Center tried to bounce dolphins' clicks off metal cylinders filled with different materials. The results showed that the features of the returning echoes were clear enough to distinguish cylinders of various shapes and contents.

Dolphins are not blessed with spectrum analysis, but they can distinguish between two objects by means of echolocation. Do they do that by choosing the echoes without knowing what they represent or do they actually perceive their shapes through the echoes? In other words, do they "see" with sound? The answer seems to be positive. Experiments conducted recently revealed that instead of associating an echo with a visual image, as in the case of Pavlov's dog (learning to associate the sound of a bell with food), dolphins can actually tell that both the echo and the image are of the same object. It seems that in dolphins, the region responsible for sight might also handle sound or at least the sounds coming from echoes.

From a different angle altogether, it seems that the echolocation beams serve the dolphins in other capacities as well. For the past twenty years or so, there has been a theory that dolphins are capable of using sound beams to stun their prey. Now, for the first time, such behavior and capabilities may have been found to be real. K. Martin and D. Herzig from Hawaii and Florida claim that dolphins use low sound beams to disorient schools of fish, damage their ears or even kill them on the spot. However, most scientists disagree and say that these beams are used only for the purpose of detecting the prey (the original use of echolocation) and nothing more.

Taste and smell

The sense of taste appears to be present in at least some cetacean species. Dolphins can detect a range of chemicals dissolved in water, and can differentiate between sweet, sour, bitter and salty tastes. The ability to taste can be utilized in a number of ways – not only to investigate food items for signs of decomposition or toxins, but also to detect the waste products of other dolphins (it is estimated that dolphins urinate every ten minutes, so a group of dolphins probably leaves a very heavy chemical trail behind it as it travels through the waters). The waste products might contain sexual pheromones, indicating the readiness for mating. They might also provide useful information for navigation, locomotion and orientation. In addition, it is believed that waste products contain chemical indicators of physiological stress, which may serve to alert the other members of the group.

Eyesight

Since they are air-breathing mammals, dolphins need to be able to see both in the water and in the air. Today, eyesight is considered to be an important tool in the lives of dolphins, as opposed to the opinion shared by many scientists in the past. From the evolutionary point of view, the eye of the dolphin developed in order to see in the air; only later did it undergo adaptations to enable it to see in water as well. One of the problems is that light travels slower in water than in air and refracts, or bends, when it passes from water to air. An eye adapted to focusing in air loses its focusing power in water. Cetaceans have overcome the problem by developing very strong muscles around the eye that can change the actual shape of the lens in the eye to suit either air or water.

Light intensity constitutes a different problem for dolphins. Light levels under water are quite low, whereas the levels outside of the water are very high. Cetaceans have developed a large pupil that can absorb large amounts of light so that they can see even at great depths. When they view objects, whales and dolphins often turn on their side to use a single eye, which can readily be moved around to provide a broad range of vision. Studies in the wild have proved that dolphins have a strong preference for yellow and red. This suggests that dolphins do possess a certain ability to differentiate between colors. People who have had the wonderful opportunity of swimming with dolphins, whether in the wild or in captivity, can attest to the way they look at objects in the water, coming close, turning on their side and "observing". They do that with humans as well, and it is certainly a unique experience to be observed by a dolphin from up close. The bottlenose dolphin's eye is capable of detecting moving objects. Unlike land mammals, its eyes are not spherical in shape, but rather elliptical along a horizontal axis, so that the objects moving into its field of vision cross a much broader area of the retina. Thus, the faster projection of a large image helps the dolphin detect food, hunt, avoid threats and coordinate movements with other members of the group. Some dolphins are capable of binocular vision, like human beings, but that varies from species to species. In that connection, many people who work closely with dolphins, such as researchers, trainers or therapists, claim that their dolphins can identify them personally when they are standing above the level of the water. However, this claim has never really been proved by scientists. The ability to recognize someone personally in the water may be a result of echolocation (that is, distinguishing between different body shapes), but recognizing a face or an image standing outside is a different matter, still to be researched and discovered. We do know that the dolphin's aerial vision improves with distance, so when you approach a dolphin from the outside and kiss him on the head, it is unlikely that he sees your face, but he certainly feels your touch.

The bottlenose dolphin has a 180-degree range of vision – forward, lateral and backward, but cannot see upward. Perhaps that is why it is observed swimming on its back; in that way, it is able see above it while

**Photo: Galit Amiel. Dolphin Reef, Eilat, Israel.
Website: www.dolphinreef.co.il**

swimming (instead of "standing" vertically in the water with its head above sea level). Another fascinating characteristic of the bottlenose dolphin is the apparent independence of its two eyes. According to some research results, it seems that while one eye sees in dim light, the other can adjust and see in brighter, stronger light. This seems to be very logical because the dolphin is often seen swimming on its side, with one eye in the water and the other outside.

Some species have the ability to look both forward and down. The Orca (also called Killer Whale, but actually a dolphin) can look upward behind its head with both eyes.

The subject of vision is particularly interesting when it comes to river dolphins. These unique dolphins are characterized by very weak eyesight – in some species almost non-existent. For instance, the river dolphin of India and Pakistan, called "susu", has no lens in its eyes. An absolute minimum of light penetrates into their dark, muddy world. However, even this helps them find their way, navigate and see large creatures approaching. The pink dolphin of the Amazon, the "bouto", has a yellow lens that may be used for filtering light in its muddy environment (see Chapter 3 for further details).

In addition to the various ways in which dolphins utilize their visual abilities, as described above, they also manifest certain behaviors that are connected to the subject of eyesight. They perform a kind of aerial surveillance that is called "spy-hopping". They "stand" vertically with their eyes above the surface of the water and then rotate their heads, scanning the entire 360-degree field.

Vision may help dolphins detect enemies, such as sharks or killer whales. It might also help them in recognize each other and differentiate between different dolphin species. In addition, a dolphin's appearance can provide clues as to its physical condition (scars, spots, shades in coloration, signs of skin diseases, etc).

Touch

Dolphins (and whales and porpoises as well) underwent a process of adaptation (i.e., millions of years of evolutionary forces working purposelessly together), the result of which enabled them to survive in the seas, oceans and rivers of this world. As a part of this adaptation, dolphins "lost" their limbs, hands and fingers, since the need for a streamlined body was stronger, in evolutionary terms, than the need to keep the limbs. Nevertheless, the sense of touch is a very important one for dolphins, and anyone who has had the opportunity of touching a dolphin will no doubt attest to the way dolphins enjoy being stroked and touched. It sometimes seems as if they cannot keep their flippers to themselves... They stroke, rub and mount each other constantly, and it appears that touch is a very important element in their social lives. In fact, captive dolphins have been successfully trained using touch as the only positive reinforcement. Through such encounters, one can really feel how sensitive a dolphin's skin is to the touch of the human hand. Their skin is not only sensitive, but also highly developed and specialized. It contains a complex system of organized nerve endings that are found in higher concentrations in certain areas of the body. These areas are consequently much more sensitive. This is true for the area surrounding the blowhole, for example,

**Photo: Galit Amiel. Dolphin Reef, Eilat, Israel.
Website: www.dolphinreef.co.il**

which contains many nerve endings that are sensitive to pressure changes. In this way, the animals know exactly when the blowhole is in the air and can be safely opened for breathing. The same applies to the areas around the eyes and jaw.

While dolphins are also sensitive to water movement and flow, we do not yet know to what extent. But apart from this tactile sensitivity, dolphins use the sense of touch in many social and sexual contexts. Dolphins stroke and touch each other with their pectoral fins or flukes, rub their whole bodies together and press their genitals against another dolphin, whether it is of the opposite gender or not. Dolphins use their tails to gently strike other dolphins (they do that with humans as well) and also use their jaws to pull them on to another dolphin's body, sometimes even leaving visible marks on its skin. Certain researchers claim that dolphins have special structures in their skin that respond to sounds (!) produced by other dolphins in the group in social, sexual or aggressive situations.

Chapter 3

The dolphins of the world

Introduction to ecology and distribution

The delphinidae is the largest and most diverse family of cetaceans in existence today. It includes dolphins and small-toothed whales that exhibit different dimensions, brain size, distributions, adaptations, diets and behaviors – from the mighty 10-meter killer whale to Hector's dolphin, which is only 1.5 meters long. According to fossil records, the age of the family can be assessed at least ten million years.

Interestingly, they are divided into two sub-groups in their nutrition: (1) the species that feed solely on fish, squid and other cephalopods, and (2) the species that feed on a more generalized food "menu" by adding other animals such as crustaceans (crabs, for instance) to their diet. The species that feed on a generalized diet are considered to be primitive (in evolutionary terms) and they are characterized by shorter and thinner snouts. Common dolphins, for example, feed mostly on fish, whereas striped and white-sided dolphins feed on a greater variety of foods. The various species also differ in body shape, flippers, dorsal fins and teeth.

Dolphins also differ greatly in their habitats. Some have adapted to salt water, some to freshwater rivers, some to the warm waters of the tropical zone and others to the cold waters of Antarctica. There are also differences in the tendencies of each species to be pelagic (i.e., to live in the open sea) or to inhabit inshore waters. Other species (such as the spinner dolphin) have even adopted a way of moving between inshore and offshore waters. In short, the family presents a fascinating variety and we are well advised to remember this fact, since the tendency to generalize can lead us to draw erroneous conclusions. Dolphins seem to be able to inhabit areas together with other species. Not only that – schools of different species of dolphins are sometimes sighted traveling and feeding together.

Another characteristic that indicates variation among dolphin species is the size of their populations. Some form huge schools of tens of thousands (such as the pantropical dolphin), while others form smaller schools, numbering only tens of dolphins or, like river dolphins, are quite solitary.

Some species are found worldwide and are widely distributed. These include the common dolphin (hence its name), bottlenose dolphins and pantropical spotted dolphins.

Among the dolphins, the Lagenorhynchus genus boasts the largest number of species, ranging from the North Atlantic to the Antarctic Ocean. The white-beaked dolphins inhabit northern waters, while the Atlantic white-sided dolphins live in temperate waters. The Pacific white-sided dolphins inhabit the North Pacific. Hourglass dolphins inhabit the pelagic waters of the Subantarctic and the Antarctic,

Dolphins Around The World

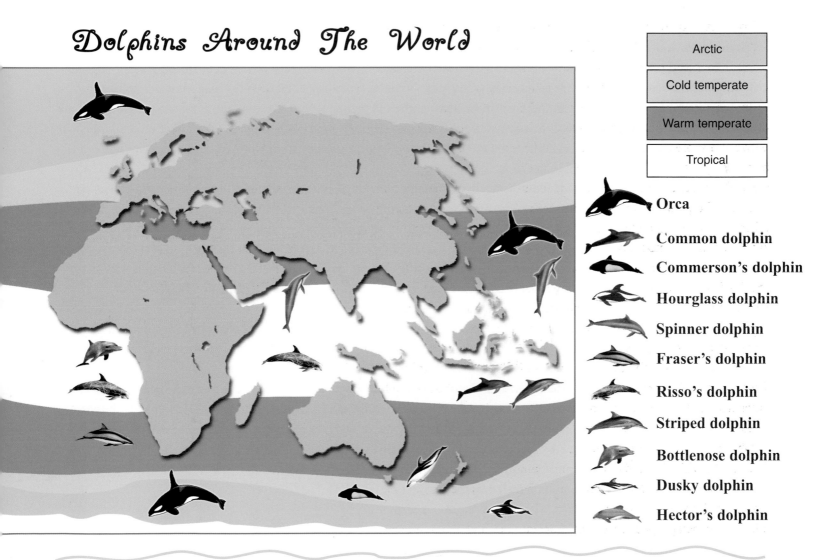

Arctic

Cold temperate

Warm temperate

Tropical

Orca

Common dolphin

Commerson's dolphin

Hourglass dolphin

Spinner dolphin

Fraser's dolphin

Risso's dolphin

Striped dolphin

Bottlenose dolphin

Dusky dolphin

Hector's dolphin

while the dusky dolphin is found in the temperate coastal waters surrounding most of the continents.

The Stenella genus (to which bottlenose dolphins belong) tend to be found in warm waters. The Cephalorhynchus genus comprises four species that are relatively small and inhabit the inshore waters of the southern hemisphere.

River dolphins tend to inhabit limited areas. The Irrawady dolphin, for instance, inhabits the inshore waters of the tropical Indo-Pacific region, ranging from northern Australia through the Indonesian archipelago and up to east India. However, it is found mainly along the Irrawady river that runs through Myanmar (Burma) from north to south. Other river dolphins are completely restricted to the river systems. These are the Indus River dolphin, Ganges River dolphin, Amazon River dolphin (the Bouto) and the Yangze River dolphin in China.

The exact location and feeding strategies of dolphin schools affect their size and distribution, sometimes within the same species. Bottlenose dolphins are a good example, since the populations in inshore and offshore waters in the same area tend to differ in body size: inshore bottlenose dolphins are smaller. This fact only adds to the already difficult task of surveying schools of dolphins, since one now has to decide whether they belong to the same species or constitute a separate species altogether. These different subgroups of the same species are called stocks and they sometimes vary in more than just body size. Spinner dolphins, for example, differ in coloration as well.

Although our knowledge and understanding of the distribution and ecology of dolphins has deepened and broadened, there is still a great deal lacking in the scientific research of these two subjects. Scientists still face many difficulties when evaluating dolphin populations and understanding the coexistence of different species, the characteristics of inshore and offshore waters, geographical migration and seasonal fluctuations. Human impact on dolphin populations and the violent interventions in their lives (i.e., things that disrupt the natural stability in their populations) have made the task at hand a more challenging one. For these reasons, there is no estimate of the size of the global dolphin population. However, with regard to certain species that have been in the spotlight during the last decade or two, there is quite a good assessment as to which are already endangered and which are facing the threat of extinction, as well as the immediate actions required in order to stop and prevent this unlawful treatment of wildlife.

Below is a more specific description of each dolphin species.

The Delphinidae family

Orca (killer whale)
Orcinus orca

This is the largest of the dolphins and is regularly mistaken for a whale due to the misleading nickname killer whale and its large size. The name might be the result of a translation error: In the 18th century, when Basque whalers saw Orcas feeding on other whales, they called them "whale killers". The translator reversed the words and called them "killer whales". Their name is misleading not only because they are not actually whales but also because they do not deserve the reputation of being dangerous and murderous, as the name implies. In fact, killer whales, though skillful hunters, do not attack or harm human beings. In Canada, for instance, wildlife enthusiasts can sail the waters of British Colombia for the purpose of watching Orcas in the wild (in other words, getting close to them). In addition, since killer whales have begun to be kept in captivity (in dolphinariums), people – especially those working with them – have been amazed to discover that those fearsome, ruthless hunters are actually very gentle, intelligent and adaptable animals. (The "star" of the movie Free Willy was a killer whale.)

Killer whales sport a very striking black and white color pattern. There are variations in pigmentation among individuals and also between different geographical areas.

Orcas inhabit tropical, temperate and polar waters, and prefer the coastal areas. Not only are they one of the world's most widely distributed mammals, but they are among the most skillful and cooperative hunters in the oceanic world. They hunt seabirds, seals, turtles, fish, sharks, dolphins and sea lions, either individually or in hunting groups.

Mating and calving seasons, which last a few months, may vary between different geographical areas.

Killer whales usually travel in small groups of no more than 40-50 individuals, unless they form larger groups for the purpose of hunting large prey, such as a whale.

When they attack large prey, their strategy is usually to approach it from several angles, immobilize it and drown it. It is possible that within a hunting group, each individual has a specific function, and successful hunting depends on the coordinated movements and cooperation of the group. They are known to employ other techniques as well. These include beating the prey into the air with their flukes (causing it internal damage), stranding themselves on the shore in order to catch pinnipeds (- 'mammals with flipper-like limbs that live both on land and in water, such as sea-lions and seals). (a technique the young are taught by the adult males), peering into ice floes in search of seals in icy regions, and sometimes even striking the ice floes in order to knock seals and penguins into the water.

Size: Adult males reach a length of between 9 and 10 meters, and females between 8 and 9 meters.

Killer whales are very dominant predators, but they have been observed and documented traveling and associating with other marine mammals without hunting them.

Orcas are famous for their magnificent aerial behavior: breaching, spy-hopping, jumping and flipper-slapping.

They are believed to possess an extra sense called geomagnetism (many other animals are believed to have it as well, including other cetaceans), which enables them to detect the earth's magnetic field – a "map" with which to navigate long distances.

Watching wild killer whales:

For those wildlife enthusiasts who dream about watching killer whales in nature, nothing can prepare you for this experience – even if you've watched hundreds of TV programs… their sheer size, magnificence and grace cannot be described in words. There are places in the world that are suitable for that purpose. Remember that although killer whales tend to remain in a certain location, they nevertheless travel long distances. They will return eventually, but since most people cannot afford to spend weeks watching whales (as the scientists do for years on end), it is advisable to be aware of timing and seasons and plan ahead as efficiently as possible.

Killer whales can be watched in organized conditions in the following places:

In the summer months, especially around June and July, two very good places in the United States for watching killer whales are: Southeast Alaska (tours leave from Gustavus, Petersburg, Seward and Ketchikan), and Washington State, San Juan Islands. In Canada, the places are Johnstone Straits (between the mainland and Vancouver Island), and British Columbia. The summer is also a good time for watching killer whales in Iceland, in the Westmann Islands and the Eastern Fjords.

Around the month of March, one of the best places to watch killer whales stranding themselves on the beach in order to catch seals is in Patagonia, Peninsula Valdes.

In the fall, northern Norway is a good spot, especially around the Tysfjord area.

Antarctica is a fantastic place to visit for many species of marine animals, including penguins, seals, whales and more. Cruises leave from Ushuaia in Argentina and Punta Arenas in Chile.

Bottlenose dolphin
Tursiops truncatus

This is probably the most familiar of all the dolphin species. The bottlenose dolphin displays a high degree of adaptation to captivity, a fact that makes it the most favored dolphin for training and research.

Group size is commonly less than 20, but large groups of hundreds have been seen as well. Much of what is known today about the general biology of dolphins comes from the study of this species,

Size: The bottlenose dolphin is a large mammal. It reaches a length of four meters at maturity. Bottlenose dolphins can be found worldwide, in temperate and tropical waters. They hunt small fish, eels, squid and shrimp and are known for their cooperative hunting techniques. (See also references to bottlenose dolphin in text).

Bottlenose dolphins are great cooperative hunters. A community of 30-40 individuals work together in a highly ritualized cooperative fishing venture.

Bottlenose dolphins are highly adaptable to changing conditions. In 1983, a very severe hurricane, "El Niño", occurred off the coasts of North and South America. Many seabirds, seals and sea lions perished as a result of a food shortage. A group of bottlenose dolphins, usually resident off the coast of San Diego, manifested incredible flexibility in coping with the new situation. The dolphins moved northward, swimming hundreds of kilometers to Monterey Bay, which offered warm waters and potential prey. Most of them stayed there until normal conditions returned and swam back to their home base. Some decided to stay in their new home.

Recently, bottlenose dolphins (among other species) were found to suffer from mass mortality. We do not yet know the causes for this phenomenon. One such event occurred in the winter of 1987, when over 750 dolphins were found dead along the U.S. coast. There is no consensus among scientists as to the cause of such large-scale mortality.

For further details and information regarding bottlenose dolphins' intelligence, hunting skills and behavior, see corresponding chapters.

Photo: Galit Amiel. Dolphin Reef, Eilat, Israel.
Website: www.dolphinreef.co.il

White-beaked dolphin
Lagenorhynchus albirostris

This species has a robust body, with a short, thick beak about 5-8 cm long in adults. Although it is dubbed white-beaked, the coloration of the beak may vary in color from off-white to gray. The white-beaked dolphin is endemic to the cold temperate zones and the subarctic North Atlantic. Around the British Isles, it is concentrated off the northern coasts of Scotland and parts of the Atlantic coast of Ireland. The white-beaked dolphin is the most stranded species found in Dutch waters. It can be sighted from the north-eastern United States to Greenland and the North Sea. This species usually strands singly.

White-beaked dolphins face a few hazards: being entrapped by wind-driven ice packs, being killed by Orcas, or becoming entangled in fishing gear.

This species frequently bow-rides waves and accompanies small boats. They are quite acrobatic and know how to leap vertically out of the water.

It seems that white-beaked dolphins travel mostly by themselves, but if they do associate with any other species, these will be fin whales and pilot whales.

They feed on squid, herring, cod and bottom-dwelling crustaceans.

Size: Adults reach a length of three meters.

Pacific white-sided dolphin
Lagenorhynchus obliquidens

Pacific white-sided dolphins have a white belly with dark to black coloration on their sides and back.

This is one of the dolphin species that enjoys accompanying ships, wave-riding in parallel to them. It prefers the open waters of the ocean, especially of the North Pacific.

It is found from the South China Sea northward, throughout Japanese waters and the Sea of Japan.

Killer whales are their natural enemies in the oceans. Human impact is hazardous mainly because of the fisheries in Japanese waters. The most notorious and tragic story associated with this species occurred on the western Japanese island of Iki. The fishermen became convinced that the dolphins were competing with them for fish and were also scaring some other fish species off, so they started to kill them. It is difficult to forget the bloody waters of Iki Island in the 1980s. Pressured by international environmental groups worldwide, the Japanese government decided to stop the killings and attempted to turn it into a site for "swimming with dolphins", which proved a success.

Having said that, this species is still the most widely caught (deliberately and as a by-catch) in the Japanese and Korean drift net squid fisheries.

Pacific white-sided dolphins are very gregarious and tend to travel in schools of tens to thousands animals.

They are known for their aerial displays – leaps, bellyflops and somersaults that are repeated dozens of times in succession.

Size: Adults reach a length of 2.5 meters, and the average length at sexual maturity is between 1.7 and 1.8 meters.

They are fast and active hunters, feeding on herring, hake, sardines and squid.

Dusky dolphin
Lagenorhynchus obscurus

The dusky dolphin is found along the coasts and in the continental shelf waters of South America, South Africa, New Zealand and other oceanic islands. Information about its numbers is not available, nor is a great deal known about them with regard to other aspects of their biology. Any knowledge we have about them stems mainly from chance observations in the wild or from dusky dolphins that have been caught in South African waters. It seems that this species does not survive long in captivity.

They have been sighted traveling together with right whale dolphins, common dolphins and pilot whales.
Dusky dolphins travel in schools of tens to a couple of hundred.
In Peru, dusky dolphins are caught by fishermen and have commercial value.
Size: The largest dusky dolphin to have been measured was 1.81 meters in length.
They feed on mackerel, sardines and squid.

Atlantic white-sided dolphin
Lagenorhynchus acutus

The most striking aspect of the Atlantic white-sided dolphin from the point of view of coloration is the white patch along each side. They also have a well-defined patch of yellow-brown that starts very narrow and widens as it stretches backward toward the upper part of their tail. This is the only dolphin with such distinct patches along its sides.

This species is restricted to the temperate zones and the subarctic regions of the North Atlantic.

They travel in large schools numbering hundreds and associate mainly with fin whales and humpback whales. Mixed herds of Atlantic white-sided dolphins and white-beaked dolphins have been observed as well. They bow-ride waves and are known to be able to travel long distances at a relatively high speed.

Atlantic white-sided dolphins strand singly or in groups (in one stranding 150 individuals were counted).

This species is faced with the dangers of human fishing (especially the use of nets and harpoons) and pollution.

Size: Adults reach a length of two meters.

They feed on herring, small mackerel, squid and other small prey.

Spinner dolphin
Stenella longirostris

Agility, jumping, spinning, speed and flexibility are all characteristics of this charming dolphin. It is observed in temperate waters in the Atlantic, Pacific and Indian oceans. Some groups seem to be pelagic while others prefer the coastal regions.

Size: Adults reach a length of two meters.

Spinner dolphins are found in tropical, subtropical and warm waters all over the world. They inhabit open seas and areas around islands. Spinner dolphins travel at high speeds and cover different habitats in a single day. During the daytime hours, they tend to stay close to the shores, where they rest, and during the night, they travel to deeper waters for hunting and feeding. During their hours close to the shore, they form groups not exceeding twenty or so, and during the night, the size of the groups increases to several hundred in number. It seems that this behavior is linked to their feeding strategies: Since they hunt fish that travel in large and dispersed schools, they need larger groups during feeding times to cover greater areas and cooperate in order to forage and hunt these fish.

Their aerial behavior marks an interesting differentiation between day and night, with their impressive spinning and acrobatic performances increasing with the approach of the darker hours. They also engage in a kind of zigzag swimming combined with jumps as they gather the whole group and travel offshore.

A fascinating phenomenon connected with spinner dolphins is their association with spotted dolphins (Stenella attenuata). It has been observed that the spotted dolphins forage and feed during the day while the spinner dolphins rest near the shore, and rest while the spinner dolphins forage offshore. This special arrangement seems to be satisfactory to both species.

Unfortunately, the millions of spinner dolphins have met their deaths in tuna nets (see Chapter 7 for further details).

They feed on squid and small fish and can dive to depth of around 60 meters.

Common dolphin
Delphinus delphis

Once considered to be a single species, the common dolphin has officially been separated into two distinct species known as the short-beaked common dolphin and the long-beaked common dolphin. It is one of the best-known dolphin species and is frequently sighted in warm and tropical waters around the world. This species is commonly featured in the art and legends of different cultures. It is easy to identify as a result of its black, ocher and gray coloring.

Size: Adult males reach a length of 2.6 meters and females 2.4 meters.

They feed on herring, sardines and anchovies, which they usually hunt during the late afternoon hours. They can hunt at depths of up to 280 meters.

Hourglass dolphin
Lagenorhynchus cruciger

This very beautiful black and white dolphin inhabits the icy subantarctic and Antarctic offshore waters. Most observations of this species have been conducted in the area extending north and south of Antarctica, between South America and Macquarie Island.

Size: Males reach a length of 1.5 meters or more. While the hourglass dolphin may be the smallest of the genus, only five specimens (2001) have yet been measured.

Striped dolphin
Stenella coeruleoalba

The range of the striped dolphin extends further into temperate regions, although it is primarily a warm-water species. It is /fairly restricted to the open waters of the ocean. Herds number between 100 and 500 dolphins.

Size: Adults reach a length of 2.6 meters and weigh up to 156 kg.

They feed on small squid and fish.

Fraser's dolphin
Lagenodelphis hosei

For a decade and a half, this species was known only from skeletal material, until it was "rediscovered" in the early 1970s.

This dolphin inhabits the warm and tropical waters of the Indian and Pacific Oceans. It prefers the open ocean and keeps well away from boats and ships.

Herds tend to be large, consisting of hundreds and even thousands of dolphins.

Size: Adults males can reach a length of 2.7 meters and a weight of over 210 kg.

They feed on squid, shrimp and fish.

Risso's dolphin
Grampus griseus

The term "Grampus" was derived from grand poisson and was applied historically to all medium-size toothed whales. Today, however, it refers only to Risso's dolphin.

It is quite easy to identify Risso's dolphins from their striking coloration – a conspicuous scar pattern on their skin that is particularly apparent on the animal's dorsal and lateral surfaces. Calves have much fewer scars on their bodies; the scars "develop" with age.

They inhabit temperate zones, from the cool to the tropical, and prefer the open oceans to the coast areas. They are most commonly found deeper into the continental slope.

Risso's dolphins travel in large schools that can consists of several hundred individuals, but small groups of a couple of dozen only have been observed as well. Risso's dolphins have been observed mixed with other species, such as gray whales, Pacific white-sided dolphins, Dall's porpoise, northern right whale dolphins, sperm whales and pilot whales.

By-catches of Risso's dolphins have been recorded worldwide. In Japan, Risso's dolphins are caught for food and for fertilizers.

Risso's dolphins are considered to be the most difficult species to capture.

Size: Adults reach a length of 4.3 meters and a weight of over 400 kg.

They are thought to feed on migrant and bottom-dwelling cephalopods.

Hector's dolphin
Cephalorhynchus hectori

This is a small dolphin with a unique and beautiful appearance. The tip of its lower jaw and the sides of its head are black, its back and sides are light brown to light gray and its belly is white. Its dorsal and pectoral fins are rounded and its flukes are very long and pointed.

Hector's dolphin is found in coastal and estuarine waters and is encountered mainly in New Zealand.

It is assumed that calves are born during the summer migration from New Zealand's south island to its north island.

Size: 50 cm at birth to 1.8 meters at maturity.

Commerson's dolphin
Cephalorhynchus commersonii

    This dolphin, with its stocky body and no visible beak, is a powerful swimmer. Its colors are very distinctly black and white – black head, shoulders, pectoral fins, dorsal fin, tail and flukes.

    Size: Adults reach a length of 1.6 meters.

    This species inhabits the cool southern hemisphere and is observed mainly in a solitary state or in group of less than ten animals. It can very occasionally be seen in schools of hundreds.

    They feed on small fishes, squid and shrimp.

Pantropical spotted dolphin
Stenella attenuata

Pantropical spotted dolphins inhabit the oceanic tropical zones. They can be found in all oceans. They are among the most abundant dolphins in the eastern tropical Pacific. School size is generally less than 100 near the coasts, but the offshore schools are larger.

The herds associate with yellow fin tuna schools and this puts them at risk because of the fishing industry.

Size: Adults reach a length of 1.6-2.4 meters. Offshore populations weigh at least 120 kg, but the ones that inhabit the coastal regions weigh more.

The Platanistidae family (river dolphins)

Ganges River dolphin and Indus River dolphin
Platanista gangetica

The Ganges River dolphin can be found along the Ganges, Brahmaputra and Karnaphuli Rivers in India and Bangladesh.

Also called the "susu", the Ganges River dolphin is remarkable for its swimming pattern. It swims on its side to allow the edges of its pectoral fins to comb the bottom of the river. Its eyes, which can only distinguish between light and dark, are very small and their function is minimal. In fact, this species of dolphin travels and feeds using echolocation only.

Its body is dark gray on the back and fading to light gray on the belly.

Size: Calves are 75 cm long at birth and adults reach a maximal length of 2.5 meters.

The Indus River dolphin lives in Pakistan and is not only separated geographically from the Ganges River species – it is in fact a different species.

The gestation period lasts eight to nine months and the calves are born in the spring.

They feed on the shrimp, catfish and carp that are found on the river floor.

The Iniidae family

Amazon River dolphin
Inia geoffrensis

This species, also known as the "bouto", is the largest of the dolphins living in freshwater rivers. It is pink and gray and lacks a distinct dorsal fin, but its paddle-shaped pectoral fins are quite distinct. Its eyes are small but functional and its beak is very long and powerful.

The Amazon River dolphin inhabits the main rivers of the Amazon system and the Orinoco Rivers of tropical South America. There are three geographically separated subspecies whose natural boundaries are mountains, but the differences are not so distinct as to divide them into different species.

They feed on crustaceans, catfish and freshwater fish.

The Lipotidae family

Chinese Yangtze River dolphin
Lipotes vexillifer

This species, also known as the "baiji", is one of the rarest in the world and its endangered state is exacerbated by the deteriorating conditions of the river. In the framework of recent efforts to rehabilitate it, large protected natural reserves are being planned for them (see Chapter 7 for further details).

Its body is stocky and the flukes are well developed. The color changes from light to dark bluish gray on its back to white on its belly.

Size: Male adults reach a length of 2.1 meters; females are larger.

The dolphin is restricted to the lower and middle reaches of the Yangtze River in China.

This species has very developed echolocation abilities since the river water is very silty and muddy in certain parts.

They feed on bottom-dwelling catfish and other freshwater fish.

Irrawady River dolphin
Orcella brevirostris

The Irrawady dolphin is pale to dark-bluish gray in color and has a robust body, bulbous head and no distinct beak. They are around 60 cm long at birth and grow to a length of 2.2 meters.

They are slow swimmers and prefer the protected environments of warm and shallow estuaries or the inshore muddy waters of the more tropical areas.

For further details about its cooperation with fishermen and its environmental status, see chapter 7 and 9.

Chapter 4

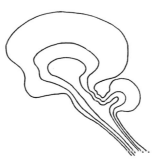

Intelligence

It is not an easy task to define intelligence in the broader, abstract sense. It is even more difficult to measure the intelligence of a particular animal in relation to primate or human intelligence. The deeper we delve into the subject, the more we realize how complex and varied it is, and how difficult and even dangerous it is to measure and determine the level of intelligence of any animal.

Some people say that it is futile to attempt to apply human concepts of intelligence to another animal that inhabits a medium so different from ours and/or functions in and relates to its environment in a different way. There is a notion that challenges the very possibility of knowing the thoughts and feelings of the person sitting next to you! So is it at all possible to learn the thought processes and feelings of another animal?

If you ask the average person about dolphins and whales, he/she will most likely mention their amazing intelligence and perhaps even other incredible abilities and characteristics. How did this idea become so deeply rooted in people's minds? A skeptic might see it simply as part of a myth that has existed in human cultures for thousands of years. When it comes to dolphins, myths about them have flourished abundantly throughout human history. However, myths always start from something, and sometimes they contain a grain or even a lot of truth. It is reasonable to assume that four major phenomena have contributed to the popularly held opinion that dolphins are very intelligent mammals. These four phenomena, which will be detailed and explained below, are the following:

- The fact that dolphins are indeed very talented performers and that their learning capacity is impressive.
- Their relatively large brains.
- Their behavior.
- The unique and intriguing rapport they seem to have with human beings.

Learning: One way in which individuals (both animals and humans) learn is by imitation, which is a natural learning process. Dolphins are frequently observed mimicking other dolphins, whether in the wild or in captivity, in their natural behavior or in training. It is amazing to witness how young dolphins (born in captivity) imitate the adults (including their mothers) in their trained display gestures. The young ones observe the adults performing and slowly start performing themselves, without the intervention of the trainers. They also mimic sounds and use tools (see Chapter 10 for further details).

Dolphins have been taught a sign language. One of the scientists who has contributed a great deal to the understanding of bottlenose dolphins' intelligence and communication is Dr. Herman from the University of Hawaii. He tested them for visual and vocal memory and tried to teach them artificial languages. One language was based on gestures and the other on sound. The experiments tested whether the dolphins can comprehend sentences or are capable of creating a new language. These experiments showed that dolphins can be taught to understand the rules that underpin languages as well as the terms of relative location in space.

Brain size: The second and one of the most important phenomena is their relatively large brain size. It is vital to understand that large brain size is not a characteristic of all dolphin species. Indeed, some species – river dolphins, for example – have quite a small brain. So when we talk about the cetacean brain, we are actually generalizing to a large extent. However, speculations and comparisons involving brain size and weight in relation to the body weight of dolphins and whales have been broadly discussed. The brain size of a bottlenose dolphin, for instance, is 1,600 grams and constitutes 0.94 percent of its body weight. The human brain weighs 1,500 grams and constitutes 2.1 percent of our average body weight. Scientists have tried to find an index that shows some link between the degree of brain development and intelligence. Research has shown that the dolphin's brain size is less developed than that of humans, but more developed than some highly intelligent primates such as the chimpanzee.

One of the characteristics of the human brain is its highly developed, complex and multi-folded frontal region, called the cortex. This is the seat of conscious control and complex thought processes. The similarity between the human brain and the dolphin brain lies in the large size of the cerebral hemispheres, but the cortex in dolphins is much thinner than in humans. Are we then to assume that dolphins are necessarily less intelligent than ourselves? Scientists' answers to this question differ. However, we can learn a great deal from behavioral experiments with dolphins in captivity or from observations in the wild.

Research in the wild can contribute to our understanding by means of observing dolphins in their natural surrounding and the behavior of the whole group. Watching a group of Orcas cooperating in hunting, for instance, clearly shows that Orcas understand the rules of cause and effect – that is, if you do one thing, another will happen as a result. They create waves high and strong enough to knock seals off ice floes in Antarctic waters. Then they hunt them in the water.

Bottlenose dolphins have been seen trying to open knots tied by fishermen at the end of their nets. This demonstrates that they understand what holds the nets together.

This brings us to the question of language and communication among dolphins. Do dolphins have a language? If so, is it anything like the languages humans know and use? These are questions to which no dolphin researcher has yet claimed to know the answer (see Chapter 5 for further details).

The fact that dolphins can be taught foreign languages and are able to comprehend sets of rules does not tell us whether they use anything similar in their own free and natural world of communication.

In metabolic terms, having a large brain is a very costly thing for an animal. When we breathe, for example, about twenty percent of the oxygen inhaled is earmarked for nourishing our large brain. Thus, in evolutionary terms, it makes sense to "develop" large brains only if it is crucial for the life of the species (i.e., the animal needs more powerful information-processing abilities), and if a delicate balance between the benefits and the costs is not only maintained, but ensures successful survival in the wild. Therefore, the question is why dolphins have been gifted with relatively large brains. Several theories have been propounded in an attempt to answer this question:

The first theory states that dolphins' large brains have evolved in order to enhance the animals' foraging skills and, more specifically, to enable them to have a mental picture of their surroundings at sea so that they can remember what to catch and where to catch it. However, some dolphin species have excellent foraging skills in spite of the fact that they are only endowed with relatively small brains.

The second theory perceives these large brains as the result of the outstanding echolocation capabilities of dolphins (see Chapter 2 for further details). In other words, great processing powers were required in order for the dolphin to cope with all the information picked up via echolocation. However, this does not explain the small brains of other dolphins and other creatures (such as bats) with echolocation abilities. Of course, there may be a difference, in that the processing and information perceived in large-brained species is more complex and vastly more sophisticated. The problem lies in studying the difference, if it exists at all, and determining whether this is the only factor involved in large-brain development in dolphins.

However, perhaps the most important contributing factor to the evolution of large brains is the dolphins' highly complex social system and communication skills among themselves. It is assumed that threats such as sharks sparked the forces of evolution to empower the brain, since group cooperation in defense against an external predator requires communication and sophisticated social skills.

It has recently been discovered that dolphins can recognize themselves in a mirror, which is indicative of highly developed mental faculties. This contradicts previous assumptions made by scientists that only human beings and the other great apes are capable of doing so. It has also been suggested that dolphins have self-awareness. Self-awareness is thought to be linked to processes of higher-order perspective-taking, including the feeling of empathy. While these abilities were once associated only with humans and perhaps apes, it now seems likely that dolphins also possess them. Recent examinations reveal that both self-awareness and empathy may originate in the right hemisphere and it is possible that, like language, lateralization plays a key role in the development of these abilities. However, scientists still have a long way to go before such conclusions can be proved.

Behavior: Observing the behavior of dolphins and their unique method of communication reveals obvious intelligence, even though it is difficult to evaluate and compare it to ours. If we had to choose one tantalizing example of hunting behavior, it would certainly be that of Orcas. The hunting methods of Orcas are famous (or infamous?) worldwide. The interesting phenomenon is that Orcas seem to have a different hunting technique for each type of prey, and the older Orcas evidently teach them to the young ones. This is culture and education in a state of constant evolution.

There are other hunting and behavior characteristics that surprise the observer in their complexity and high evolvement and the reader is referred to Chapter 6 for further details.

If we combine all these characteristics – large brains, complex society, mutual help, learning from experience, teaching their offspring – it all adds up to the conclusion that an Orca is an intelligent animal.

However, it is very difficult to measure and compare, and we only have our subjective point of view of intelligence to go by

Rapport with humans: The fourth phenomenon is the curious and mysterious connection they seem to have with human beings (see Chapters 8, 11 and 12). Dolphins have become one of the animal species that most appeals to humans. While they certainly exhibit a unique gentleness toward and rapport with people, is that necessarily indicative of some special powers of communication or intelligence they possess? I do not believe that this fact alone is relevant to the issue of intelligence. It is a fact that chimpanzees, gorillas and other intelligent apes and primates are very intelligent. They could continue living quietly and undisturbed, completely ignorant of human beings, if it were not for the latter seeking them out (regrettably, usually for negative purposes that lead to nothing but their decline and suffering). From an emotional point of view, however, we tend to feel that because dolphins seem to have a special rapport with us, it undoubtedly provides us with an indication of their intelligence. (In other words, the existence of the rapport would seem to indicate that humans and dolphins share some sort of similar intelligence.)

Scientists today agree that dolphins are indeed very intelligent beings. Professional disagreements and controversy stem from the questions regarding dolphins' degree of intelligence, the similarity between their intelligence and ours, and the degree of development of their communication (i.e., whether they have an actual language) and whether we could ever really know and understand it from our (limited) human point of view. In addition, we should not forget that dolphins' evolutionary path of life on earth was different than ours.

Chapter 5

Communication

Animals communicate with each other in many different ways. Communication is a very complex subject to study at all levels and stages of evolution and the living world, since it is not always clear, straightforward or external. In fact, the opposite is true. In the animal world at large, communication occurs through chemicals (for instance, pheromones), visual signals (for instance, sexual organs), external behavior (for instance, the mating dance of the male peacock) and probably in many other ways of which we are still ignorant.

Dolphins are more limited in their range of communication methods because of their streamlined bodies, expressionless faces and the fact that conveying communicative chemicals through the medium of water is much less efficient than in air.

On the other hand, sound travels better and further in water. Consequently, dolphins rely to a large extent

Photo: Galit Amiel. Dolphin Reef, Eilat, Israel. Website: www.dolphinreef.co.il

on the vocal world in their communication and have evolved amazing capabilities for producing and deducing a variety of sounds. Vision plays an important part, as do the different behaviors of the individual and the sense of touch.

It has been observed that dolphins alter their behavior following certain sounds, which indicates that these are in fact communication tools. This does not mean that these sounds are a language, as we know it. It does not mean that dolphins talk to each other as human beings do. However, from various studies that have been conducted on the subject, it can be concluded with high probability that at least some of the grunts, whistles, groans, clicks and slaps that dolphins produce serve to convey information from one individual to another. It is important to bear in mind that the description of the various sounds relates to what we hear, and not necessarily what the dolphins hear. Because their sense of hearing is so different than our own, the dolphins' ears might perceive these sounds entirely differently. For example, dolphins are able to perceive individual clicks that are fired off very rapidly, whereas we hear them as one continuous mew. In addition, dolphins' auditory range far exceeds our abilities (that is, they can hear much higher frequencies).

Generally speaking, the sounds produced by odontocetes can be divided into two main groups: (1) the pure-tone whistles and pulses – the sounds that are made out of echolocation beams (see Chapter 2 for further details); and (2) sounds emitted under special behavioral circumstances, such as groans, barks, grunts, etc. However, echolocation beams may also play a role in communication – in other words, they may not be used solely for catching prey.

The clicks and whistles are produced in a series of air sacs in the soft tissue below the blowhole in the dolphin's head. Pressurized air is forced out into a sac below the blowhole. The lower-frequency sounds are less focused, whereas the higher ones are directed forward and out of the head through the melon – the waxy lens-shaped structure in the dolphin's forehead.

Interestingly enough, not all dolphins and porpoises whistle. Hector's dolphin and porpoises do not whistle at all and it is probable that neither do Orcas. The only likely explanation for the difference lies in the fact that whistling dolphins belong to species that form large and stable herds, whereas those that do not form such herds tend to travel in small groups only and are less gregarious.

Since whistles are characterized by low frequencies, they travel greater distances in water than pulsed sounds and do not overlap in frequency with the echolocation clicks, so the two sounds can be emitted and perceived simultaneously. In order to explain the evolution of the whistles, some researchers have put forward the theory that whistles enhance the contact between the members of a foraging group.

It has been documented that when dolphins arrive at a familiar place, they emit more sounds than usual. Sometimes, as in the case of spinner dolphins in Hawaii, the dolphins whistle at the highest rates when they return to their resting place in the shallow bays. In addition, activities that excite them, such as bow-riding or accompanying a boat in the open sea, generate numerous whistles as well.

It has also been noted that captive dolphins whistle at a high rate when feeding times are approaching. Moments of stress are other very important times when whistles feature significantly.

The question that arises pertaining to whistles is why has evolution "favored" the development of such sounds, when they clearly introduce a factor of risk into the dolphins' lives. Whistles can be heard for long distances and many other sea animals, including predators, can hear them. It might be too dangerous to whistle when a calf, for instance, is left alone without its mother. The answer probably lies in the benefit of knowing which dolphin just whistled. Mother and calf, for instance, need to maintain close contact for a couple of years. As the calf grows up and its confidence increases, it begins to explore its environment, gradually swimming away from its mother for longer periods of time. The mother needs to know where her baby is and needs to be able to call him and find him at all times. An amazing phenomenon that has developed in dolphins is a signature whistle. It is now known from studies on bottlenose dolphins in captivity that each dolphin has its own unique and specific whistle – its very own signature whistle (see chapter 6 for section on 'Signature whistle' for further details).

Even if a dolphin alters certain aspects of the whistle, such as its loudness or rapidity, it still remains its own unique whistle, since it maintains its special contour. That means that it is highly possible that dolphins are able to identify the "voices" of their group members and distinguish them from those of strangers. It also offers the fascinating possibility that there are various degrees of bonding between the dolphins in a group. In other words, a dolphin might be closer to a particular individual (what we might call "friendship" or perhaps a different kind of mutual relationship) and less connected to another. From different situations in which the dolphins emitted sounds that were duly recorded, it has been observed that dolphins respond differently to the calls of a familiar dolphin than they respond to the calls of a stranger. This might suggest that social bonds are strong within the group in dolphin society.

Thus, in addition to the important function of the whistle as the signature or "name" of an individual dolphin, there is evidence that whistles not only vary, but are emitted in consistent ways in different behavioral contexts.

Beside whistles, dolphins produce other sounds that constitute their complex system of communication: clicks and other pulsed sounds. It has been found that these sounds accompany specific behaviors, and are therefore an important part of communication. For instance, the bottlenose dolphin produces a "popping" sound characterized by its low frequency when it is herding females. The sound is associated with aggression and threat. Before and just after mating, bottlenose dolphins produce a kind of yelping sound. Some sounds, such as screaming and growling, are evidently used when the dolphin is angry.

If we are looking for dialects (similarly to dialects in human languages) or what appears to have developed as such in certain species of dolphins, we can find them among killer whales. Orcas form pods, and each pod can consist of a few subpods. Each subpod can be separated from the others for days, weeks or even months. The Orcas have developed their own unique dialects that are distinct to each pod that lives separately from the others, geographically speaking. This phenomenon is unique in the animal kingdom, since we usually find vocalizations to be the same for a genetically identical population. (see chapter on Behavior for further details).

killer whales are probably capable of conveying a certain situation or mood, identifying each other and warning others of danger. Of course, it is highly likely that we haven't come close to knowing the whole spectrum of their communication capabilities. (This is true of dolphins in general, not only of killer whales; in fact, it is probably true of most animals.)

Dolphins can create other sounds that are not really vocal in order to communicate. They are occasionally seen to slap their tails, flippers or even their heads or the entire bodies against a surface or the sea floor. This might convey anger or disturbance to other dolphins. When dolphins emit a big spurt of bubbles or one big bubble from their blowhole, it is also indicative of surprise or some other reaction.

It still remains to be seen whether dolphins possess a highly developed language of their own, and whether it is in any way similar to anything we are familiar with. Scientists require a great deal of endurance, patience and wisdom if they want to reveal more clues about what dolphins are saying to each other as studies go deeper and deeper into the world of communication.

Chapter 6

Behavior

Hunting behavior and techniques

Dolphins hunt in many different ways. Each and every member of a group can spend its time seeking its own prey and hunting it by itself, but under certain circumstances, specifically when the prey is found in a solitary state or in huge aggregations, dolphins utilize complex cooperative hunting techniques for the benefit of the entire group. Herds of dolphins are quite often observed engaging in cooperative hunting – an essential activity for their survival. Apart from the necessity to find food and the obvious advantage of increasing efficiency by foraging and hunting together, dolphins form such groups in response to threats – namely predators.

In some instances, a lone dolphin cannot target huge schools of fish. There are clues that lead us to believe that dolphins use marine topography as a guide to navigation and food-finding. They "hear" different landmarks by listening to the increase in noise around them that indicate where schools of prey have gathered. This is one form of behavior that requires their unique sense of echolocation (see Chapter 2).

It often happens that large groups of dolphins swim in complete silence, not uttering a single sound. This might help them listen out for sounds of potential prey. Common dolphins, spinner dolphins and spotted dolphins often form hunting groups that extend many kilometers. Sometimes the prey is swimming quite deep under the surface and the dolphins must surface for air and dive down to the fish as quickly as possible in order to keep up with them. Another technique involves dividing the herd into two functioning parts: the larger part swims in parallel to the coastline but further out to the sea, while the second part, consisting of two to four dolphins, swims to the coastline itself, looking for prey. When the smaller group detects fish, the rest of the dolphins swim together toward the coastline and surround the fish from both sides.

Bottlenose dolphins employ a clever method in order to maximize their foraging efforts: they follow northeastern Pacific pilot whale schools. By swimming just above the whales' heads because of their inferior diving capacity, they feast on the fish that are forced-gathered by the whales.

The same association is found between schools of yellowfin tuna, which number hundreds of thousands, and groups of spotted and spinner dolphins. The tuna follow the dolphins as the two species hunt for the same source of food. This has had very unfortunate consequences for the dolphins, because when fishermen realized that they could follow yellowfin tuna schools by detecting groups of dolphins, they simply hunted them together in large fishing nets, imposing a virtual death sentence on thousands of dolphins. Many ecological and environmental organizations have tried to prevent this tragedy from recurring by teaching fishermen alternative tuna fishing methods and by encouraging the general public to buy tuna only from companies that guarantee and supply "dolphin safe" tuna (specially marked on cans of tuna and available worldwide).

Dusky dolphins herd large schools of anchovies to the surface, which serves as their border, and swim under and around it. Then, in turn, each dolphin swims forcibly into the spherical mass of anchovies, emerging at the other side with its mouth full of fish. A "guard" dolphin immediately chases back anchovies that try to escape from the swirling ball. This technique cannot be utilized for too long; in fact, it is only good for a couple of minutes, and then it's up to each individual dolphin to catch as many anchovies as possible while swimming through the ball.

One of the most skillful hunters in the dolphin world is undoubtedly the killer whale or Orca (see Chapters 3 and 6 for further details). There are two characteristics that enable the killer whale to be such

an amazingly good hunter: its massive size and strength and the its extraordinary cooperative behavior. Since they are such skillful hunters, killer whales enjoy one of the most 40 varied diets of all cetaceans. They hunt seals, birds, penguins, other dolphins and whales, fish, and so on. The interesting phenomenon is that Orcas seem to have a different hunting technique for each type of prey, and the older Orcas evidently teach them to the young ones. This is culture and education in a state of constant evolution. In the Antarctic, part of the pod shakes resting penguins and seals from their ice floes right into the mouths of the pod members; they take turns to dive into caves in which seals are hiding, so that when the seals surface (for air), there is always a member of the pod there to catch it. In Argentina, they swim near a shore inhabited by sea lions, seals and young elephant seals. They search for a suitable seal and once the unfortunate victim has been chosen, they rush to the beach, strand themselves on it, and seize the seal in their mouths. The second part of this hunting method is not easy either, since they have to get off the land and return to the sea. Even so, they manage to wriggle back to the water with their prey. It takes several years for a young Orca to learn this technique because it is a very sophisticated and difficult method and one that certainly requires creative intelligence.

Aerial behavior: Leaps and jumps

There is no doubt that one of the most beautiful sights when it comes to dolphins is the way they gracefully and effortlessly jump and leap out of the water. Sometimes the whole group or the majority of it can be seen performing one leap after the other. Scientists speculate that beyond the mere "fun" involved in such behavior (animals are certainly known to engage in playful activities for fun and pleasure rather than for social or behavioral reasons), dolphins perform these leaps and jumps in order to survey the area using aerial vision. Aerial vision is probably most important in food foraging. These jumps may enable them to get a feel for their whereabouts. If they spot sea birds or fishermen in the area, it might provide them with clues as to the location of prey. Dolphins often leap when pursuing a school of fish. This is because they are trying to get to the surface to breathe and back into the water as quickly as possible, and their momentum almost causes them to fly through the air. It is possible that some of the dolphins in the group serve as guards or scouts – in other words, they leave the herd to explore other areas in search of fish. When they locate the prey, they signal to the others to join them in feeding. Some scientists suspect, however, that such altruism is actually indicative of individual dolphins that are so eager to find food that they want to be the first to get hold of it.

In addition, some scientists believe that dolphins actually communicate with each other through aerial behavior, and are able to point out to other members of the group where they can find food.

Dolphins engage in a peculiar behavior called spy-hopping. They rise vertically out of the water, head first, often letting their eyes or their entire head reach just above the surface. Then, they rotate 360 degrees, observing their surrounding.

In addition to finding potential food, aerial behaviors may assist dolphins in spotting danger – for instance, killer whales or sharks. Spy-hopping may serve as a way not only to seek prey, but to avoid falling prey themselves to a predator.

Aerial behavior may help dolphins coordinate their movements as large groups, since they are usually seen leaping while traveling together. Leaping may enable the dolphin to catch a glimpse of the other members of the group and their relative location.

Interestingly, aerial behavior might serve as a clue to the identification of an individual. Just as humans who are trained and experienced in watching dolphins can identify a particular dolphin just by its aerial jumps (since each dolphin has its own unique jumping "style"), so it stands to reason that members of the group can identify other members by observing their jumps. Even more: dolphin experts today assume that dolphins use their visual aerial sense to read the gestures and displays of their group members – a real body language, so to speak. As the dolphin's body is devoid of many external features and facial expressions,

they have to rely on the language of the entire body to convey a particular message to other members. Every little movement – such as moving the pectoral fins, shaking the head, opening the mouth or bending the back into an S-shape – may convey something to another dolphin.

Social behavior

Dolphins are highly social animals. However, in order to investigate their social contacts and behavior, we first need to examine some basic facts, such as group size. It might be surprising to learn that scientists do not yet possess even this basic information. Not only do group sizes vary greatly, but little is actually known about the group size of some species. It can range between practically solitary individuals, such as some of the river dolphins, to groups of thousands. In addition, it is important to remember that a huge group numbering thousands is not necessarily a stable one. In other words, it gathers for a specific activity (for example, feeding) and can then divide up into smaller groups. Researchers who wish to examine social behavior have to identify individual dolphins in a group and determine whether some of them form stable relationships (and of what nature) or are only an "aggregation" of dolphins with certain temporary feeding or mating purposes. Although this is one of the most difficult tasks in researching dolphins in the wild, it did not deter the single-minded scientists who undertook to tackle it back in the 1970s.

In evolutionary terms, being a social animal means that living within a group is more advantageous than living in a solitary state. The overall cost to the individual of living within a group is outweighed by the benefits it derives. Such advantages can include protection against predators, cooperative hunting and reproductive behavior.

As a general rule, in dolphin society, males are more dominant then females. The communication of dominance occurs more reliably through the perception of the submissive individual than through the behavior of the dominant ones. When a particular dominant dolphin cruises by, the subordinate dolphin that happens to be in its path will flee or just move away. Scientist have found definite indications of dominance or a "pack order", even though it is not as strict as in other mammals. It seems that some animals within the group have never been molested by others and are more aggressive and less fearful. The oldest and/or largest male in the group is usually the most dominant. During mating seasons, the dominant male is observed swimming with one particular female for periods of several weeks. The female is submissive toward him and swims with him constantly, only leaving for short feeding breaks. There is usually a "second-best" dominant male or female after the first and then the group breaks down into sub-groups: older females, then young males, and lastly the youngest members of all.

Females often form groups with their female relatives in the group in order to facilitate the tasks of foraging, feeding and protecting themselves and their young. The males dedicate their time to finding and hunting prey and competing among themselves. There are several parameters that influence and determine the strength and duration of bonds between females. These are, among others, age, status, reproductive cycle and kinship in the group. Females may swim together and socialize for two or three generations and form a network of contacts that may endure for many years. However, we know very little about this. Females belonging to the same network of contacts may be able to offer support to the unfortunate females that get involved in chases by males (see "herding a female", below). An additional female support system exists when one of them is rearing her young. Other females may offer help in the form of "baby-sitting" and enable the mother to rest. In addition, females serve as "aunts" to other females with infants and assist them in protecting their young.

Some species of dolphins, like the bottlenose and the dusky dolphins, form societies that exhibit fascinating similarities to chimpanzees and spider monkeys. These societies are characterized by a certain fluidity, that is, a system in which size and membership often vary on a daily basis. Some members enter the group while others leave it. This is not an indication of the absence of a stable relationship between members. Mothers and their calves form one of the most stable and basic units in dolphin society. It has been observed that even males may form close ties with other males, foraging, traveling and socializing together for many years.

Male dolphins may collaborate in behavior known as "herding a female", which happens when two or more male dolphins chase a lone female – sometimes for long distances and long periods of times. This is not limited to chasing only; there is a lot of aggression involved and the herded female will sometimes emerge from a chase bruised all over, with many tooth-marks on her skin. Researchers are still trying to get to the bottom of this behavior and find out what happens once the chase is over. Are the males trying to force themselves sexually on the female? Are they trying to prevent her from copulating with other males? Are they warning the female to stay close by and not leave the group? Are they trying to impress the female or each other? There are many open questions here.

As was mentioned and stressed before, a major setback in dolphin research, particularly in the field of their social behavior, is the difficulty involved in studying free-ranging animals in the open sea or ocean. Of course, studies have been conducted on dolphins in captivity, but the fact that they are a closed group that lacks the fluidity typical of many of the dolphin groups in the wild renders this research unequal to research performed in the open sea. However, the close and virtually personal ties between certain dolphins in the group can be analyzed and studied in addition to vocal and behavioral communication, which, together with data from the wild, can help us put all the pieces of the puzzle together. However, we still have a long way to go in our quest to understand sophisticated dolphin societies, not to mention simpler creatures or other life forms.

Killer whales – a special case for social and hunting behavior

Killer whales (Orcinus orca) have a worldwide distribution, both in inshore and offshore waters. The distinct external features of these magnificent animals are characterized by black and white coloring, and (as opposed to other dolphins) the difference in appearance between males and females is easy even for the untrained eye to see: males are much larger than females and their dorsal fins are twice the size of those of the females. This was very helpful in the research of killer whales resident in British Colombia, Canada. The geographical stability of the communities and the relative ease in differentiating between males and females made it possible for scientists to investigate the structure of their social lives with the aim of understanding it better.

The core of killer whale society is the mother and baby. This basic maternal group does not consist only of the mother and her infant, but also of older females that spend their entire lives close to their descendants – offspring, grandchildren and so on. The maternal groups create the pods. Pods can create subgroups and they can (but not always) create a population that lives in the same area. In British Columbia, it was discovered that populations inhabiting the same area separate into sub-groups that differ in their specific preferred location and in the size and level of stability of the group. Each such community inhabits a different location: one in the north, a second in the south, and a third that is transient and appears only occasionally, moving in between the two stable communities. Each community in turn divides further into pods, which consist of dolphins that are probably related to each other. Each pod can contain a different number of dolphins, ranging from a single couple to dozens of dolphins. Only pods from the same community will associate with each other. Some of the pods may contain only females or only young males, but there are also mixed-sex pods. The stable communities do travel around, and in fact, each travels freely along at least 500 kilometers of coastline. Interestingly, each community (two resident and one transient) has a different dorsal fin. From afar, they look identical, but from closer up, there are some variations in their shape.

Research both in the wild and in captivity has shown that Orcas possess a very rich vocal repertoire that is used in communication. It appears that each pod has evolved a unique dialect that is distinct and different from that of other pods. This is unique in the animal kingdom, since we usually find vocalizations to be the same for a genetically identical population. Orcas use vocalizations to coordinate group behavior and maintain contact with all members. It has been suggested that although these "dialects" vary among the pods, an Orca from one pod would be able to communicate with an Orca from another pod because they still share many identical communicative vocalizations. However, since the dialects are not conveyed in sequences that resemble syntax, scientists do not regard them as languages as we know them. Also, they do not contain any calls or sounds that are associated with any particular behavior, object or prey – that is, what we call words. Nevertheless, killer whales are probably capable of conveying a certain situation or mood, identifying each other and warning others of danger. Of course, it is highly likely that we haven't come close to knowing the whole spectrum of their communication capabilities.

Mating and reproduction

The mating of killer whales has never been observed in the wild. However, it seems that males leave their pod to look for suitable females in other pods. Alternatively, mating may take place when two pods congregate. A super-pod may contain more than 100 Orcas and they stay together for a few hours every time. If mating occurs during these meetings, the newly pregnant females return to their respective pods and raise their young there. This means that the males may never see their offspring and certainly do not help the mothers raise them.

When the baby is born, it measures 2-2.5 meters in length – very impressive for a newborn! The calf is able to swim – albeit a bit awkwardly at first – as soon as it is born. It stays close to its mother for at least a year and is fed highly nutritious milk (usually under water). Only at the age of 1.5-2 years does it start feeding on solid foods and begin to hunt with the pod. However, it takes him a few more years to wean itself of its mother's milk and protection.

Killer whales spend their entire lives within their families or pods. The baby always stays with its relatives in the pod, and that is why males have to search for females in other pods – to avoid mating with their own sisters or other genetically close females.

Orcas live quite a long life, similar to that of humans. In the wild, males live 50-60 years and females 80-90 years. In captivity, it is a fact that killer whales do not reach the end of their natural life span, and die by 35 years of age.

Sexual behavior

Reproduction is the ultimate goal of evolution – to create offspring that will perpetuate the genetic heritage through endless generations. Animals strive to reproduce and their behavior, socializing and feeding strategies are all means to that end.

As mentioned in the section on social behavior above, the study of dolphin reproduction in the wild is a very difficult task since the act of mating is seldom seen in the open seas. In the wild, when one observes a male dolphin approaching a female with his penis erect, one might attribute this to sexual or courting behavior. However, even a scientist observing dolphins from the possible nearest point cannot tell whether the male has penetrated the female, let alone whether he has ejaculated inside her. In addition, dolphins are very sexual animals, that is to say, they engage in a lot of sex-related behavior (for example, they touch each other's genitals, masturbate, and so on). Thus, one can witness a great deal of contact between the two genders, and analyzing which behavior is reproduction-intended or just sex play becomes a confusing and frustrating process. However, studies conducted on bottlenose dolphins and killer whales in captivity have provided scientists with a great deal of information regarding these dolphins' sexual behavior, courting, mating and parenting.

Male Bottlenose dolphin touching the genitals of a female

It is still important to remember that despite all the insights we have gained from such studies, the sexual (or any) behavior of dolphins in captivity may not reflect the entire range of behaviors that exist in the wild. The facts may be quite different. However, it is reasonable to assume that the truth lies somewhere in the middle and the importance of researching dolphins in favorable conditions, preferably in semi-captivity, is unquestioned.

Mating systems

In general, dolphin reproduction is seasonal, although it varies from species to species. Some have one distinct breeding season while others have one or two or even seven peaks of sexual activity annually. However, it is not always that simple. It is clear today that environmental factors such as water temperature, availability of food, and so on influence seasonal reproduction in certain dolphin species. Perhaps there are additional variables of which we are not yet aware. For instance, bottlenose dolphins – one of the more studied species – breed during the months of May to July in warm climates. This can be different in colder regions in either the northern or the southern hemisphere. Since gestation lasts for over a year, dolphins actually mate during the birthing period.

In general, one can say that the mating strategy "chosen" by dolphins over millions of years of evolution is polygamy, that is, males copulate with many females (as opposed to the system of monogamy in which a couple remains "loyal" to each other all their lives). Large males exhibiting vigorous behavior are able to defeat other males in order to win females. However, in some dolphin species, the situation is more complicated. The female bottlenose dolphin, for instance, has seven estrus cycles annually. This is significantly linked to their mating systems because the polygamous strategy of the males can clash with the female's "chosen" mating system – seven estrus cycles in one year. Let me clarify this. The polygamous dominance of a male over the female depends upon his ability to monopolize the female and be the one that wins her when she is receptive and most likely to conceive and perpetuate his genetic heritage. This strategy can succeed in species with one estrus cycle during the year, that is, one cycle in which the male is either successful in his efforts to win a female or is forced to wait until the next year. But in the case of the bottlenose dolphin, females are sexually available seven times a year, and this reduces the chances of a male monopolizing one female, since she mates with many males many times all year around. However, as we go deeper into the understanding of animal societies, we realize how sophisticated they are. In the case of the bottlenose dolphin, what advantage does the female have by being so receptive almost all year around? It might give her a valid claim for paternity and so the risk of her baby being killed by a male, as happens in other mammal (primate) societies, is very slim indeed. The males are less likely to threaten the infant because they have mated with the mother and could actually be its father. Thanks to this strategy, the female may increase the chances of her infant to survive to maturity. This is only one plausible theory, however, and there may be other factors and strategies involved, which have not yet been taken into account.

Is it a male or a female?

It is worthwhile describing the general sexual anatomy of dolphins since it is crucial to the understanding of their sexual behavior. As mentioned in the Introduction, the adaptation of dolphins to the seas, oceans and rivers of the world made it vital, in evolutionary terms, to achieve a streamlined body. That involved the modification of the external genitalia as well. Dolphins' genitalia are completely hidden in the body except during sexual activity, when the males' erect penises are clearly visible outside their bodies. Consequently, it is very difficult to differentiate between males and females on the basis of a superficial examination – with the exception of such differences as length of body or size of fins. The penis is retained inside a prepuce (unless it is erect) whose opening is a slit, which is quite similar to the females' genital slit. The only conspicuous external difference between the genders is the distance between the anus and the genital slit: in females the distance is very short – in fact, it almost seems to be a continuation of the anus. In males, the distance is much longer. In addition, the female has nipples on either side of the genital slit. These nipples are hardly distinguishable, since they are always retained in a tiny mammary slit and protrude only during suckling. The mammary glands themselves are well hidden beneath the blubber. It goes without saying that the fact that the external difference between the genders is so negligible adds to the already difficult task of studying the sexual behavior of dolphins in the wild. How can we tell whether it is a male touching a female or vice versa? From the moment scientists began to recognize dolphins and identify them by specific external characteristics, giving each one its own name, serious research could then commence. Later, a new and revolutionary method was developed, whereby a dart was shot into a particular dolphin in order to collect genetic information (see Chapter 10 for further details).

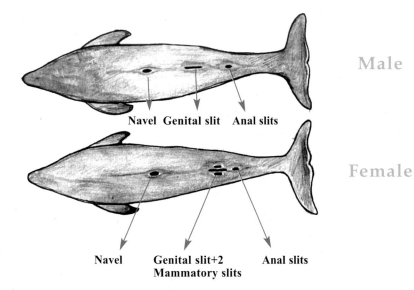

Male

Navel Genital slit   Anal slits

Female

Navel   Genital slit+2   Anal slits
             Mammatory slits

Sexual maturity

The age at which male and female dolphins become sexually mature is still unknown in some species. However, in the case of intensively studied dolphins such as the bottlenose dolphin, these data are available. The earlier a dolphin matures, the more potential it has for reproduction and for producing offspring. Sexual maturity is closely linked to physical size, and that in turn might be linked to the availability of food in the dolphin's environment. In comparison to whales, many of the odontocetes take a long time to reach sexual maturity. Female killer whales, for example, reach maturity when they are between eight and ten years old, and bottlenose dolphins are around twelve years of age when they give birth for the first time.

Erection of an adult Orca

Courting and copulating

With regard to dolphins (and other marine mammals, for that matter), it is still an interesting question how males actually identify and locate receptive females in the water. In land mammals, pheromones and/or secreted chemical signals are used in the sexual communication between genders. In addition, these mammals display conspicuous sexual organs that indicate a readiness for mating. Whether dolphins also utilize such methods is a question that remains pretty much unanswered. It is possible, of course, that dolphins taste the water for signals regarding female secretions, but it is more likely the behavioral change of a female and/or a vocal signal that she emits that indicates her readiness to mate. Bottlenose dolphins have been seen inspecting the females' genitals. They do that by swimming on their side, with their body bent diagonally so that the head is lower than the tail and placing their beak near the female's genital area (see illustration on page 87). They might be able to test the area for minute changes that occur during the female's estrus cycle and/or taste any chemical indicators in her urine.

One of the indicators (for the human observer, at least) that mating is about to begin is the evident excitement manifested by both genders. Neither males nor females can stop touching, rubbing and / mounting each other. The male then swims toward the female and positions himself in front of her, performing one of the bottlenose dolphins' most typical acts of courting behavior: he bends his body into an "S-curve" with his head up and his flukes down. After holding this position for a few seconds, he repeats this action a couple of times. It also

the s-curve position of a male Bottlenose dolphin

depends on whether the female welcomes or ignores his approaches. If she persistently shows signs of indifference, the male may withdraw and give up after a while. If she is responsive to the male's advances, the "S-curve" may be followed by further mutual touching, rubbing, hugging and stroking. It is very beautiful to watch the dolphins engaging in this "foreplay", since it makes us realize just how amazingly tactile these animals are. It is important to keep in mind, however, that their acts of touching are not always gentle and tender. Dolphins have been seen taking their partner's whole head [!], flipper or genitals in their mouths! Sometimes one of them leaps up into the air, and, upon his/her return to the water, is greeted by the other one's open mouth.

While this sex play and courting behavior is going on, anyone diving in water near the couple can hear the cacophony of sounds they emit. The male produces a series of high-pitched yelps every time the female wanders away, and does not stop until she returns. Then, the male approaches the female from the right side and rolls over, penis erect, bringing himself close to her genital area. If the female agrees, she rolls on her left side and presents her genitals to the male, while swimming more slowly. He then slides his penis into her, making a few thrusts. A few moments later, they go their separate ways. Copulation has been recorded to last between 3 and 10 seconds in bottlenose dolphins.

Males fight for supremacy in some species of dolphins, whereas in others this battle is almost nonexistent. Male bottlenose dolphins, for example, males make a considerable effort to win females.

Interestingly, some cetacean species use a completely different approach to achieving genetic supremacy. Instead of fighting off potential competitors aggressively, they are endowed by nature with larger reproductive organs, that is, testes and penises. In species that employ this kind of competition, which is called sperm competition, the females mate with more than one male and the males that gather around her are not particularly aggressive toward each other. In fact, one male was once observed waiting patiently for his turn while another was copulating with the female. Many smaller dolphins have relatively large testes, which is perhaps indicative of the importance of sperm competition. However, this should not be taken as a general rule. Bottlenose dolphins have large testes in relation to their body size, but they still fight for females. It has been found that in bottlenose dolphins, sperm production rises dramatically during the mating seasons. This means that in biological terms, sperm production is costly, so it should not be wasted in seasons during which mating does not take place.

Giving birth

The birth process of any mammal is a stressful one for the mother, whether on land or at sea. However, it must be particularly so in the open waters, since the newborn emerges directly into the water, where it can drown or lose body heat rapidly. In contrast to land mammals, dolphin calves are expelled tail first rather than head first. The birth or labor is a quick process in dolphins (and whales alike), since the infant must swim quickly to the surface for its first breath directly after the umbilical cord is cut, otherwise he might die of anoxia.

Dolphins give birth to only one infant at a time. Twins have been recorded, but they are extremely rare. The mother dolphin has an immense task in front of her – to feed, protect and teach her baby everything it needs to know in order to survive, and she will put all her energy and time into it for a long time (one year at least). It is therefore reasonable to assume that in the case of twins, one of them – probably the weaker one – will have to be abandoned (as happens in some species of mammal, including the Great Panda of China). Evolution selects those with better chances of surviving and reproducing in their turn.

It is extremely rare to observe dolphin births in the open sea, but births have been witnessed and record-ed in places where dolphins are kept in captivity. It is an amazing event – a true celebration of life – to watch the birth of any animal (including humans), but even more so when it comes to dolphins. First of all, in order to be able to watch the birth, one needs to be in the water, snorkeling or diving. So one is already a guest in a different world from one's own, a guest in the world of the dolphins. Second, the birth of a dolphin is a very delicate procedure. The mother needs to ensure that the infant is emerging properly, which she does by feeling the movement of the water around her and coordinating the emergence of her baby with the streams and currents. After this, she must quickly ensure that her newborn swims quickly to the surface for its first breath, so she helps it by nudging it with her beak. Third, the fact that the tail emerges first in dolphin births is completely alien to us –different than any other births we may have wit-nessed. It is amazing to watch the tail emerging, followed by the rest of the smooth and shiny body. A moment later, a small baby dolphin is out there, swimming instinctively to the surface. Finally, another amazing phenomenon to observe while a birth is taking place is the behavior of the rest of the group. It seems obvious that the other members of the group are there for the mother. They try to assist her, surround her to protect her from predators and threats (in the wild), swim around her in great excitement, and, when the infant emerges, some of the "aunties" help the mother direct it to the surface. In cases of newborn infants that are too weak (and do not stand a chance) or in cases of stillborn births, these "aunties"

have actually been observed taking the infant to the bottom of the sea and holding it there. Presumably they are estimating its chances for survival and act accordingly. To watch the group's excitement and awareness of the birth is a fantastic experience that encapsulates and conveys directly to the eyes of the observer just how social, communicative and intelligent dolphin societies are.

An amazing phenomenon: in dolphin's birth, the tail emerges first, followed by the rest of a smooth and shining body.

As in the case of a breach birth in humans, it can happen that the infant turns inside the womb and emerges head first. This is not easy for the mother. It might take her days of hard and stressful labor to finally give birth. In some places where this has been observed, it was clear that the whole group surrounding the mother understood her difficulty and constantly swam around her anxiously, inspecting her genitalia and trying to keep up with her erratic swimming.

What happens after birth is the subject of the next section.

Maternal behavior and the first stages of life

Young calves can be easily recognized in the wild, both by their appearance and by their behavior. Newborn calves are much paler than their mothers and also have marked vertical lines, or "fetal folds", on their flanks. These can be seen quite easily, even from afar. It seems that the embryo inside the mother's womb is large in relation to its mother's size and it crumples up inside her womb. These folds are the result. After the newborn has surfaced and filled its lungs with oxygen, the mother uses her tail and beak to steer it to where she wants it to position itself – beside and in front of her dorsal fin or near her tail. Sometimes it looks as though the infant hardly needs its mothers' guidance in positioning them – it seems to find its way very quickly and learns to ride along the waves generated by her movements.

In the same way as baby apes cling to their mothers, so this hitchhiking is vital to the baby dolphin's survival. It needs to maintain constant contact, especially during the first few months. The calf probes its mother's belly for nipples and she positions herself with her belly toward it and causes her nipples to protrude. The calf grasps the nipple with its jaws and a stream of milk is released into its mouth in response to its touch. Because they are underwater, feeding cannot go on for long periods at a time, since they have to surface for breath. For this reason, the calf suckles close to the surface, but still underwater, so that both mother and baby can take frequent breaths when they need to. The milk is actively ejected into the calf's mouth by muscle action, so that the transfer of milk to the calf is faster – an advantage of underwater nursing.

Every now and then, the mother has to stop feeding her infant for a while because she has to breathe or because of some other distraction. The reaction of a hungry baby to interruptions in feeding, that is, when the mother actually retracts her nipples, is sometimes characterized by frustration and anger. The infant can even become quite aggressive toward its mother in its attempt to regain the nipples (or anything else for that matter). The tireless stubbornness of the calf can lead to two possible reactions on the part of the mother: when she has had enough, she either teaches it an aggressive lesson or lets it have its way. Both reactions have been witnessed.

Dolphin mother's milk is rich in fat and calories for the rapid growth of the baby, which feeds on nothing else for many months. It is worth mentioning that even when the baby reaches the stage at which it starts to feed on tiny fishes, suckling may still go on, albeit less frequently. This is the stage at which the infant begins developing a taste for something other than mother's milk, and it occurs between the ages of six and eight months.

The infant then learns how to hunt and catch small fish, a process that is taught by the mother and which is conducted mainly by playing with the prey. This activity occurs when the tiny fish jumps and tries to escape from the dolphin's mouth. The young dolphin lets it escape and then chases it again, only to catch it again and so on until it actually eats the fish. A similar play-learning process has been observed in kittens (hunting a mouse, for instance) and other mammals. In the case of dolphins, the foods that serve as the calf's "toys" will eventually become a part of its diet. In addition to teaching her baby how to catch prey, the mother wants it to acquire new tastes so that it will start eating other foods. She does so by tearing a fish into small parts, removing the big bones and the head, and presenting her infant with the small and soft remains. She takes great care to remove the dangerous parts that might harm the calf's tender digestive system.

Another interesting behavior manifested by young dolphins has to do with echolocation and the need for them to train themselves (with their mother's help) and gain experience in using it, since it certainly demands a great deal of acquired skill. For instance, a calf might track a fish, try to focus echolocation sounds on it, try to catch it and try it again if he is not successful (which is the case with the very young). With time and training, these young dolphins will develop into mature and skillful hunters and the females amongst them will, in their turn, teach their young the art of hunting.

The mother and her infant swim together a lot. This fulfills two purposes: strengthening the bond between the two of them and training the calf to swim and breathe. By teaching the baby the skill of swimming and breathing fast, she may actually be training it to escape from predators or other threats whether or not she is present.

The mother dolphin has already invested a lot of energy and time in gestating the infant for many months and giving birth to it. This single infant is going to be attached to her for over a year. It will receive protection and nourishment from her, and she will teach it how to hunt, dive, explore and socialize – as well as how and of what to be careful. The mother-child unit is the closest tie in dolphin societies and one of the strongest ties holding the group together. The mother's experience is highly important in dolphins. It has been witnessed in captive dolphins that mature, older and experienced mothers have an easier time rearing their calves than first-time or young mothers.

In the case of bottlenose dolphins, mothers and calves tend to have a very long relationship. The young dolphin may stay in the close proximity of its mother for six years and even more. The mother keep their calves close to their sides, push them away from new or unfamiliar objects, get them out of the way when other animals plunge into the water after a jump, and in general, watch them constantly.

One factor that determines how long they will be so close is the mother's next birth. In the wild, the chances that a female will have longer intervals between births are greater than in captivity, since in the latter case the number of females is stable, fixed and probably, in most cases, smaller in comparison to the number available for males in the wild. It has happened that females in captivity give birth every other year and sometimes even in consecutive years. This means that the amount of time and depth of bonding between mother and calf may differ significantly between free-ranging dolphins and captive ones. However, we do not know this yet. The calves, on the other hand, sometimes seem to want to escape from their mothers' iron grip and protection. As time passes and their confidence grows, they start developing their own unique individuality and may try to do some dangerous things, such as swimming far away to places with which they are not yet familiar or simply explore their environment curiously, encountering its amiable aspects and sometimes its dangerous aspects, too. That is all part of growing up. Generally speaking, although the young calf is already spending time on its own exploring the area and gaining confidence, it still returns to rest under its mother up to the age of at least two. When the mother becomes pregnant again, however, she pushes it away from her.

Signature whistle

Mother and calf need to maintain close contact for a least a year. As the calf grows up and its confidence increases, it begins to explore its environment, gradually swimming away from its mother for longer periods of time. The mother needs to know where her baby is and needs to be able to call him and find him at all times. An amazing phenomenon that has developed in dolphins is a signature whistle. It is now known from studies on bottlenose dolphins in captivity that each dolphin has its own unique and specific whistle – its very own signature whistle. When the calf is born, the mother whistles a specific "name" for her baby. Presumably, her repetitive whistling during the first days of her calf's life is a form of acoustic imprinting on her infant. The whistles differ in frequency, tone, form and duration. To our human ears, they sound very high-pitched. They can last between a fraction of a second to more than a second.

Here are three Spectrograms of such Signature whistles:

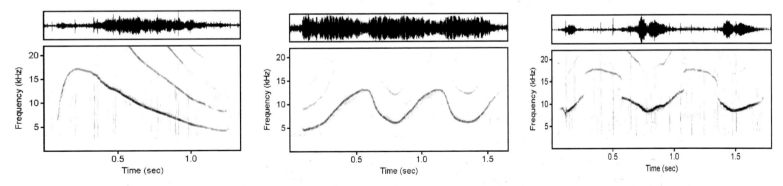

Three Signature whistles of Dana, Dicky and Luna (from left to right, respectively). Dolphinlab, Eilat, Israel.

When the mother whistles this specific name, the calf can recognize it from among all the different sounds in the water, and will be able to find her. Signature whistles serve as communication tools not only when the mother needs to find her calf or vice versa, but also in maintaining contact even when they are far apart.

Similarly, the baby develops his own signature whistle, which allows his mother to know his whereabouts. Interestingly, not only the mother knows and recognizes her baby's whistle, but also all the members of the local community. Thus, socially speaking, the entire group is constantly aware of the whereabouts of its young generation and perhaps even shares responsibility for them with the mothers. It is also possible that if the mother cannot find her calf, for instance, all the other "aunties" and group members will be able to help her find him, since they know his "name". The calf does not produce his whistle right from the start. He must practice it again and again until it is perfect and stable, because this signature whistle will characterize him for the rest of his life.

A baby Orca sucklimg from his mother

Mothers protecting their young

Mother dolphins are extremely protective of their young, since the environment is full of hazards and threats that put the tender and vulnerable infant at risk. The group itself can also provide protection in the form of a sort of a physical "wall" surrounding the pair. It is quite easy, even in the wild, to observe the protective behavior of the mothers in a group of dolphins. When the infants are only two weeks old, they become daring and leave their position alongside their mother. The mothers tolerate this behavior to a certain extent only, permitting a certain amount of "naughty" behavior, but always retrieving the baby if it dares to venture beyond a certain point.

Whether in the wild or in captivity, it is a sad and tragic part of life that young calves sometimes do not make it to adulthood. The mother's reaction to the death of her baby has been witnessed both in the wild and in captivity. It is obviously painful for the mother, who was so attached to her baby, to let it go. One mother was observed carrying her baby's dead body on her head, refusing to let it go. Only after some time had elapsed did she let the body fall to the bottom of the sea, never to return to it again. Another mother was observed pushing her dead calf's body through the water. Yet another mother (in Sarasota) kept on lifting her infant's dead body and dropping it, whistling all the while. This ritual continued for an hour and a half until two males came and chased her away. After that, she never tried to find her baby again.

Captive dolphin mothers with young that already feed on fish always seem to put their infants' welfare before their own. They ensure that the babies have eaten before they do.

When the young dolphins grow up and reach the age of three or four, they must break away and begin their own independent lives. They may remain in the same group with their mothers, but without their close guidance, protection and authority.

The information regarding free-living dolphins and the manner in which separation takes place is limited. However, it seems that in the case of bottlenose dolphins at least, young females tend to leave gradually, that is, they leave and join other groups and then return for a short visit and so on until total separation has been effected. Young males appear to form close alliances with other males and stay with them, paying only brief visits to their mothers. Interestingly, when a mother gives birth to a new baby, she calls her older offspring to announce the birth. Perhaps it is a sort of a family reunion and/or a celebration.

Without a doubt, dolphins are very social animals and the mother-calf unit is one of the strongest pillars supporting it.

Altruistic behavior and mutual help

Evolution has molded animals to behave altruistically toward their relatives in proportion to the cost of the act involved. This is defined by how close they are genetically and by the benefit/s that can be derived by the performer of the altruistic acts. Altruism is well known in the animal kingdom, and it seems that dolphins are among the most altruistic animals. Since early times, sightings of dolphins assisting their group members have been documented in many locations and in species throughout the world. Dolphins have been known to help mothers during the birth process and immediately afterwards. In the case of a stillborn calf, other dolphins immediately take the dead infant away from the mother, while in the case of a healthy birth, they remove the placenta. Dolphins have been known to throw themselves into the middle of a confrontation between a hunter (for instance, a human fishing boat) and a dolphin that is fighting for survival. They have been sighted supporting a distressed member of the group on the surface. This can occur when the dolphin is weak, old, sick or injured. They do it by holding the sick dolphin up with their flippers, and supporting its head so that it will not drown. While engaging in this type of behavior, the assisting dolphins neglect their own needs, that is, they do not feed or hunt. In fact, they themselves are barely able to breathe and do so rapidly every few moments.

There is no doubt that this kind of altruistic behavior is highly developed in dolphin society and people find it very exciting and moving to witness it.

It is certainly understandable for dolphins to behave altruistically toward members of their group, whether this is instinctive behavior or genuine awareness of a friend's or relative's difficulty. However, dolphins not only engage in that kind of behavior out of a feeling of kinship with the members of their group. They have been seen to behave in this manner with other species as well – more specifically, with human beings. Dolphins have been seen coming to the rescue of drowning swimmers, carrying them along the surface of the water to safety. This is one of the phenomena that gave rise to one of the most popular myths surrounding dolphins, which states that as a result of a very special feeling dolphins have toward people, as well as their kind, good nature, they always help them out. This unusual tendency to behave altruistically toward members of other species and genera is really a puzzle.

The question is whether this is mainly a beautiful myth that has developed from anecdotal sightings or a natural behavior that is typical of dolphins among themselves and with human beings as well. If this is indeed a natural behavior, another question arises immediately. Do they behave in an altruistic way instinctively (that is, did this behavior evolve because its outcome is more beneficial to dolphin society in evolutionary terms than if it did not take place), or does their very high level of communication and social bonding lead them to a conscious (almost moral) act of mutual assistance?

We already know that dolphins manifest a very high level of cooperation, whether in hunting, educating and protecting the young, navigating, and so on (see sections on social and maternal behavior in this chapter).

Some scientists have tried to explain it by saying that these behaviors are instinctive and automated, that they are nothing but stereotyped responses to signals of distress. However, the problem is that in many of the cases, the behavior was not at all stereotyped. It was highly improvised and tailored to each and every case. In addition, it has been observed in species that are not surrounded by close relatives all their lives. Even when the behavior remains within the limits of displaying altruism toward their mates, the dolphins do not behave in a stereotyped manner; they seem to be completely aware of the circumstances and improvise accordingly.

The following incredible case is an example of altruistic behavior that was recorded by a hunting boat: A pilot whale was shot by fishermen and just as they were about to carry it aboard after it drifted toward the boat, two whales suddenly emerged from the water on either side of the dead animal and dragged the body away from the boat with their snouts. In order not to be seen by the hunters, however, they pressed the body down and disappeared with it into the water, vanishing completely. This behavior is not typical of whales or dolphins. They usually carry the animal in distress on the surface. Here, adapting themselves to the situation and understanding the circumstances, they had to behave differently, and they did.

Aggressive and playful behavior

The reason for these two separate behaviors to be included under the same heading is that the line separating them is sometimes quite thin, and each behavior contributes to and nurtures the other in the early stages of life.

Play is a very important aspect of behavior in almost all mammals, including humans, particularly as a part of the development of the young. Sometimes the difference between playful and aggressive behavior is difficult to identify and it is quite easy for the inexperienced eye to confuse the two. Watching two young lions playing with each other seems just like a fight, but on closer examination, their teeth are not exposed and their body language is not aggressive. Mammals and birds, be they young or adult, all play. Animal behaviorists claim that play may be as important to the life of an animal as sleeping and dreaming. It clearly has benefits for the animals: it fosters the healthy development of the young, determines (among other parameters) the social standing of each individual, and aids in developing strength and coordination, coping with new encounters, and learning about the environment and each other. In fact, if young mammals are deliberately prevented from playing, their development becomes abnormal.

From observations conducted on many species, scientists have recognized a few play behavior patterns. One of the most common is play-fighting and chasing (involving wrestling, hitting, biting, chasing, etc.), which is typical of kittens and puppies, as well as of human children playing chasing games. Kicking, leaping and twisting form another pattern, and the third is object play, which is playing with a certain object

(balls, rocks, sticks, etc.) – one of the most common patterns in animals and humans.

Dolphins are no exceptions to the above behavior patterns. They are considered to be real lovers of play – both in their early lives and in adulthood. They are constantly observed playing, either alone or together. They play-fight and chase: young dolphins play-fight with each other in what sometimes seems like an aggressive fight. They chase each other endlessly and at high speed, sometimes leaping through the water and breaching into the air during the chase.

Leaping and bow-riding: This is characteristic of all dolphins, whether young or adult. It is actually one of the most typical dolphin sights – dolphins leaping through the water, breaching it, bow-riding the waves as they accompany passing ships. In the open seas or in captivity, dolphins definitely seem to enjoy riding the waves in the same way as humans get a thrill out of driving fast cars, surfing or flying.

Play-object: Young dolphins can spend long hours every day playing with an object they find in the water: balls, stones, a piece of seaweed, a piece of plastic or polyethylene, and even small harmless animals, such as turtles. In captivity, dolphins have been seen carrying a piece of polyethylene on their head (which can be dangerous because it is liable to block their blowhole) or tossing objects in the water, just like children throw balls. When I was researching dolphins, I spent long hours playing with one of the young dolphins called Nana. She used to love playing a game with seaweed: She would watch my hand and produce echolocation beams as I pulled off a piece of seaweed that grew on the wooden platform. Then, I would throw the seaweed into her open mouth. She loved chasing it in the water, only to catch it and swallow it. She would then swim quickly back to me for more.

Young dolphins are frequently observed using food (fish) as a toy. A dead fish is useful for coaxing a live fish out of the rocks, only to be snatched away at the last moment. They also love balancing the fish on their snouts, dropping it and catching it again. They do this over and over again. Such games sometimes end with an adult, hovering nearby, catching the fish and devouring it. The disappointed young ones swim away without any protest and turn to some other activity. In captivity, older and young dolphins often make use of objects that have been dropped into the pool/tank. The young dolphins are often the ones who initiate the games, with the adults picking them up and joining in.

The price that young mammals risk paying when they are completely absorbed in play is increased vulnerability to predators. Dolphins in the wild are quite vulnerable from the ages of three to five because it is at this age that they start feeling more independent and confident and they are liable to play their games a bit too far away from their mothers' watchful eyes. It is really amazing to watch dolphins play. They invest a great deal of energy and creativity in their games and seem to be completely absorbed in them.

As mentioned above, they love playing with objects and particularly enjoy playing with real animals that share their habitat. They seem to treat these animals probably like some kind of toy: turtles are good for pushing around, while fish and eels can be chased and dragged along.

Dolphins are also notorious for their sex play. They can be seen trying to mate with anything that looks the least bit animate, including turtles, eels and various objects. Sex can also be a way to express aggression. This can be seen when one alliance herds, harasses and mounts another in an aggressive manner. Groups of killer whales engage in rough play that involves erections.

As opposed to the myth surrounding dolphins (namely, that they are very gentle, good-natured animals, that assist people in trouble), in real life and within dolphin society, they can, in fact, be quite aggressive. Dolphins use external signs and body language to express anger. Their threatening gestures include opening their jaws wide, spreading their pectoral fins or nodding and shaking their heads with gaping jaws. If a bottlenose dolphin wants to threaten another dolphin, it faces the other dolphin, opens its mouth and bares numerous sharp teeth, sometimes with its back arched and its head bent down. This is a very common threatening gesture in the animal kingdom. In addition, a dolphin may slap its tail, head or flippers against the surface of the water in order to indicate its feeling of annoyance or irritation. Dolphins are very tactile animals, which means that they enjoy touching each other and love being scratched by people. However, not all touching is friendly, and they are occasionally seen fighting each other in a surprisingly savage way. Sometimes two dolphins face each other and scream, growl and even bray at each other. One of the most serious manifestations of aggressive dolphin behavior is hitting an opponent with a tail. In killer whales, this has been known to be more dangerous than biting.

Aggression leaves its marks and scars, and these can be seen on a dolphin's skin when one takes a closer look: multiple scars, wounds, tooth marks and skin lesions. Of course, these can also be the result of other threats such as other predators, human impact, pollution, and so on, rather than aggressive behavior.

Strandings

To the best of our knowledge, it was Oppian, in the second century AD, who mentioned dolphin strandings for the first time. This is a beautiful description of a dolphin stranding, perceived by Oppian as the way dolphins choose to end their lives when they feel that death is near:

This other excellent deed of dolphins have I heard and admired. When fell disease and fatal draws high to them. They fail not to know it but are aware of the end of life. Then they flee the sea and the wide waters of the deep and come aground on the shallow shores. And there they give up their breath and receive their doom upon the land; that so perchance some mortal man may take pity on the holy messenger of Poseidon when he lies low, and cover him with mound of shingle, remembering his gentle friendship; or do haply the seething sea herself may hide his body in the sands; nor do any of the brood of the sea behold the course of their lord, nor any foe do dishonor to his body even in death. Excellence and majesty attend them even when they perish, nor do they shame their glory even when they die...

If we want to understand this phenomenon, we have to identify the two basic kinds of strandings: dead strandings and live ones. The first kind of stranding occurs when the corpses of dolphins (and whales, for that matter) that have died of natural causes (for example, old age or disease) or man-made environmental causes (for example, pollution) are washed ashore. Although most of the bodies of dead animals sink to the bottom of the ocean, some are carried to the shore by the currents. The second kind of stranding, in which living dolphins and whales find themselves stranded on the beach without being able to return to the sea, is the one that has attracted so much attention in recent years. This is because the phenomenon of living dolphins and whales stranded helplessly on the shore is not easily explained and does not seem to be natural in any way; it is certainly not a natural way for dolphins to end their lives.

A long list of causes has been put forward to explain this alarming phenomenon, some of which are non-scientific guesses:

𝔠 The dolphins enter a shallow area close to the shore in order to rest or rub their skin, and become trapped on the shore.

𝔠 In shallow waters, their ability to perceive sonar signals is weakened.

𝔠 They succumb to a primitive instinct to find safety on land.

𝔠 They suffer from disorientation-inducing brain infections due to pollution.

𝔠 Parasites affect their sense of balance or echolocation abilities.

𝔠 The dolphins actually take their own lives intentionally, that is, they commit suicide.

Sandy, shallow beaches confuse their sonar echoes.

𝔠 The noise pollution emitted by various ships and boats blocks natural, balanced reception of echolocation signals.

𝔠 Ear parasites prevent the proper reception of sonar signals.

𝔠 The dolphins are actually attempting to use ancient migration channels that are now blocked due to geological changes.

- Population pressure.
- Pollution caused by man.
- Radar signals that interfere with dolphins' vocal sonar and communication.
- Earthquakes that occur on the ocean floor.
- Storms that affect their navigational skills.
- The dolphins misread the "magnetic-topographic maps" that help them navigate the shallow waters close to the shore.

The characteristics of live strandings depend very much on the social nature of the species involved. In other words, species that travel in large groups tend (if they do so at all) to live strand in large numbers, whereas dolphins that travel in small groups or spend most of their lives in virtual solitude, live strand individually. If we compare the rate of stranding events in offshore and inshore dolphins, we see that the former tend to live strand more than the latter.

Live strandings are actually quite rare. In England, which has kept records of strandings for the past 80 years or so, 137 live strandings were recorded between the beginning of the 1920s and the end of the 1980s, out of a total of 3,000 strandings (the others being dead ones). This proportion is the same in other places in the world, and is not unique to the British coasts.

From postmortem analyses of live stranded dolphins that died on shore, scientists have been able to eliminate some of the plausible explanations listed above. For example, ear parasites were not found in most cases, nor were their brains found to be suffering from damage. In addition, out of all the dolphins found stranded in the UK, only two-thirds were found on the sandy shores that are thought to confuse sonar echoes. Some places where dolphins were found stranded have never altered geologically, which rules out the possibility that dolphins travel according to some ancient memory of routes. The idea of suicide as a plausible explanation seems quite unlikely. Of course it has never been tested or seriously researched (and the question is, of course, how to begin investigating such a topic).

Resting or rubbing in shallow waters is not typical dolphin behavior, and although dolphins (especially

Orcas) do tend to use such areas as "rubbing grounds", this has never been seen to culminate in strandings. In other words, dolphins know how to enter and leave shallow waters easily and unharmed.

If earthquakes were the cause, we would expect to find more live strandings in places that are more sensitive or prone to them than in areas that are not. This is not the case, however.

Dolphins travel and navigate with the help of the magnetic and topographic maps of the earth, and it seems reasonable to attribute the cause of their unfortunate strandings to this. Whales and dolphins use the total geomagnetic field of the earth as a simple map and also as a kind of "clock" that measures their progress and position along that map. They actually use the relative differences in the total field, which is not uniform, but locally distorted by the magnetic characteristics of the geology beneath it. Dolphins (and whales) seem to travel along the "hills and valleys" formed by these relative differences. They travel in parallel to the contours and do so in a very special way: they keep the higher platform on their left and the lower one on their right, just like walking along a sidewalk with one leg on the sidewalk and the other on the road. The movement of the continents has produced a series of almost parallel magnetic hills and valleys that resembles a topographic map full of "roads" or "freeways". The problem is that these "roads" do not end at the seashore, but continue on to the land itself. Thus the dolphins, traveling along these "topographic roads", might follow them up on to the land, as a result of which they become stranded. This explains why offshore species tend to live strand more than inshore species: offshore species are less familiar with navigating near the coasts, that is, with the "roads" that continue to the land. Inshore species might have experience and knowledge of these dangerous roads and refrain from following them right on to the beach.

It is possible that not all the dolphins in a group will follow the road without realizing the consequences. It seems likely that strandings are in fact "road accidents"; the dolphins stranded on the beach definitely look shocked and perplexed and always need assistance to get back to sea. However, these errors in following roads on to the land do not happen all the time (if they did, we would see many more strandings). There is probably another cause that leads these unfortunate dolphins to make such mistakes. Scientists believe that the cause is the "daily geomagnetic clock" of the fields through which dolphins travel. It has been discovered that the total geomagnetic field fluctuates regularly every day and the dolphins pick up the clues it provides every morning and every evening (in other words, similar to dawn and dusk). In this highly regular routine, there could be some irregular events caused by solar activity that occur and interfere with and/or break the normal pattern. These irregular events disrupt the dolphins' reading of the "clock". This means that if they "calculate" their traveling time – and hence the distance – from point A to point B, they might get it wrong and swim directly on to the shore instead of to point B because of some disturbance. It is not yet certain whether these events are wholly or partially responsible for live strandings. We do not know how many times, if at all, dolphins have found themselves stranded and been able to get back to the water at the last minute. It is important to mention that of all the hundreds of thousands of dolphins that live in the seas and oceans worldwide, only a small percentage gets stranded, which is indicative of their excellent innate skill in finding their way around.

There is still much speculation with regard to the magnetic map-reading ability of dolphins and whales. How do they manage to perceive these magnetic forces? There is mounting evidence showing that the dolphins' retina is highly sensitive to small changes in magnetic fields, so that might be the answer, but science still has a long way to go to understand this amazing phenomenon.

Astonishingly, dolphins that were assisted into the water again have been witnessed trying to make their way back to the shore! The reasonable explanation is that they were so disoriented, exhausted, shocked and aware of their still-stranded group members that they want to swim back to the shore. It takes a lot of effort, patience and energy to help stranded dolphins back into the water.

Sadly, it is not always possible to help stranded dolphins. By the time rescue teams arrive at the site in order to rescue the animals, it may be too late. The dolphins stranded on the beach may die of shock, too much time out of the water, exhaustion, overheating or stress.

Can we prevent the strandings of dolphins and whales? Some places in the world seem to experience more strandings than others. For the people living near some coastlines (such as in Cornwall, UK), memories of dolphin strandings are a part of their local maritime history. These places are better able to ready themselves for such occurrences and arrange rescue teams as quickly as possible.

In other places, where strandings are rare or have never occurred before, there is a need to form organizations that will study the correct plan of action to implement in live strandings so that they can monitor and supervise such events. Not only will this help dolphins in their hour of need, but it will also help in gathering information about the species and distribution of dolphins and whales in the area.

Do dolphins sleep?

One of the most intriguing questions in biology and the behavioral sciences – equally fascinating in humans, mammals or any other order or species – is sleep. I have always been interested in sleep, whether as a dream-conscious person, as a researcher in a sleep laboratory or as a lucid-dreaming explorer. This is part of my reason for electing to research the nocturnal behavior of dolphins. Our knowledge of sleep in humans and animals is very limited. The central, most basic questions such as: Why do we sleep at all? Why do we need to dream? What is the function of the different sleep stages? and so on still lack answers. When it comes to marine mammals, our knowledge of their sleep behavior, patterns and physiology is even more limited, and scientists are still pondering basic questions that have already been answered in the case of other mammals.

Mammals that live on land, such as humans, can afford to "lose consciousness" and turn their senses off (although not entirely). Animals can hide in the forest, among treetops or in holes in the ground. Humans can lock the door when they turn in for the night. In that way we can secure ourselves from predators. The sleeping dolphin, however, must cope with two crucial problems: the first is breathing and the second is predatory sharks and other potential threats.

Since dolphins breathe through their blowholes, they must come to the surface of the water in order to perform this respiratory act. The blowhole closes when the dolphin submerges itself again. The physiological control over breathing in sea mammals is therefore more complex, and there is no way a dolphin can allow itself to doze off and let water enter its blowhole or cause any respiratory dysfunction. In addition, the dolphin must remain alert to any potential predators.

Evolution has come up with an amazing, ingenious solution to these problems: dolphins sleep with one of their hemispheres awake at all times. This means that half of their brain is awake, functioning and alert while the other is asleep. They then switch sides to let the other hemisphere sleep. Russian scientists seem to have been the first to record brain waves in dolphins and discover that dolphins actually have several sleep stages, as do humans. During stage three, half of their brain is active while the other is asleep, even though it is still sensitive to various sounds. Dolphins do not sleep full nights as we do; they are better described as taking naps of different lengths – during the day as well as at night. Their sleep behavior can be divided into two main patterns: they sleep while slowly surfing in circles on the water, or dive slowly to the bottom of the sea, rise up, breathe and dive in again in repeated cycles. The question of whether these patterns are common to all species or whether different conditions (for instance, river, sea or ocean) influence them remains unanswered since most observations of sleep behavior have been performed under conditions of semi- or full captivity. When dolphins rest, it becomes difficult to approach them, and it is also not advisable. Nobody likes being bothered while resting, do they? If approached while resting, dolphins will sometime try to avoid the disturbance by swimming around it or diving under it. A whole group can disappear from sight within seconds if disturbed.

If free-roaming dolphins that have not fed for a few days or are resting are disturbed by humans, they might react by avoiding them and sometimes even by becoming irritated. Unfortunately, that sometimes happens when wild dolphins get close to the shore and are constantly bothered by people, often with motorcycles or motorboats, even though the dolphins show obvious signs that they prefer to be left alone.

Chapter 7

Dolphins and the environment

The waterways of the world have not escaped the process of destruction wrought by human hands. The oceans, rivers and seas are constantly deteriorating, even though awareness is growing and attention is being paid to the most pressing issues. Almost every ocean or sea and some of the largest river systems of the world provide a home for one dolphin species or another to live in. As these habitats disappear as a result of pollution, dam-construction, exploitation for tourism and entertainment, fishing and hunting, the dolphins find themselves losing their rightful home. And that is only the beginning of their problems. Awareness of these crucial issues can help us discover how we can change, help, correct and prevent things that can harm the environment and the dolphins living in it.

Most of the Western countries do not hunt dolphins directly. Other countries still kill dolphins either for meat or because fishermen perceive them to be a competitive element in their area. Japan, for instance, hunts Doll's porpoise and bottlenose dolphins for their meat. There is some indication that along South American coastlines, dolphins are caught because locals use their meat for fishing bait- it is not even used for their own consumption as meat.

Another growing problem, especially for coastal dolphins, is simply traffic. In some areas, water traffic has become very heavy and crowded with motorboats, large ships, yachts, sailboats, jet-skiers and so on (as a result of tourism, recreational facilities, industry, ports, etc.). Dolphins have been sighted with bruises and scars on their skin due to injuries caused by propellers and other parts of the vessel.

It is not only the physical presence of sea traffic, it is also the noise it generates. Scientists surmise that the noise may have an impact on the dolphins' hearing and echolocation capabilities. It might distort the signals passing among the group members, thereby interrupting their communication. If their communication is affected, it is reasonable to assume that their behavior and reproduction will be impaired as well.

Water sport facilities are also a source of major concern for dolphin protectors near coasts. Not only are the fast jet-skiers dangerous, but also the behavior of some of the drivers. They frequently chase the dolphins around and attempt to catch them. This is certainly not the right way to communicate with a group of dolphins that approach humans, and everything must be done, education-wise, to prevent the abuse caused by such negative human–dolphin interactions.

However, the most alarming problem this earth is facing, and which people are trying to cope with, is pollution. This problem is all-encompassing and global in its magnitude. Moreover, it affects all living things, plants and animals (including humans) acutely. Not only is it acute but also chronic, to use medical terms, since pollution starts at a certain point and continues for generations through the endless food chain, and stubbornly stays there until the earth is given a chance to cleanse itself and regenerate.

The most indiscriminate killing device used at sea up till now was employed quite frequently in the 1980s. Monofilament nets that extend up to a distance of 60 km are suspended like curtains from floats, entangling every living thing that happens to swim by. The nets are then hauled aboard ships, the fish caught are stored away and all the unwanted catch – including dolphins – is discarded. In the 1980s, in order to harvest 100 million squids to satisfy the enormous national appetite of Japan, Taiwan and South Korea, nearly 40 million other animals belonging to over 100 species were entangled in the fishing gear where almost all of them perished. A United Nations resolution banned commercial drift nets in 1993.

One of the major threats to dolphins, which is fortunately receiving worldwide attention and is being successfully minimized, is tuna fishing. Spotted and spinner dolphins are followed by schools of yellowfin and skipjack tuna that number hundreds of thousands. The tuna follow the dolphins because the two species hunt for the same source of food and the tuna have learned that dolphins with their echolocation abilities are much better at spotting the prey. The dolphins don't really mind, but once fishermen learned that they could follow schools of yellowfin tuna by detecting groups of dolphins (which is easy because of their dorsal fins), they simply hunted them together in large fishing nets called purse seines. This technique was introduced in the 1950s by the tuna fishing industry. The first thing they do is search for dolphins, since they are accompanied by schools of tuna. Once dolphins have been sighted, huge nets, 900 to 1,400 meters long and up to 130 meters deep, surround them (with the tuna underneath) and allow neither to escape. The fishermen then haul the whole catch on to the ship, killing thousands of dolphins in the process. In response to worldwide attention and pressure from international environmental groups, tuna fishing companies had to change their ways if they wanted to sell any of their tuna products.

By boarding fishing boats, the National Marine Fishermen Service (NMFS) has estimated that between 1959 and 1972, a devastating 4.8 million dolphins were killed. What a tragedy.

Protective legislation was introduced and new quotas were decided. In 1984, it is estimated that between 32,000 and 39,000 dolphins were killed, and in 1985, the number was 55,000. It is too difficult to control and supervise all tuna fishing companies around the world, and unless an international organization is established to prevent it completely, there will still be dolphins unfortunate enough to end their lives like that. Many ecological and environmental organizations tried to prevent this tragedy from recurring, and they did so first of all by teaching fishermen alternative tuna fishing methods. According to the new procedure used today, called back-down, which was developed in the 1970s, the skiff pulls the ship to one side, and the skipper backs it away from the net. The motions produced cause the far end side of the net to dip below the surface of the water, allowing the dolphins to escape. The fishermen were strongly advised and encouraged to help the dolphins that were caught to escape. The general public was urged to

1

Fishermen's boats approaching Tuna fish and Dolphins

2

Fishermen encircling both Tuna and Dolphins with net

3

Boats isolating Tuna fish and pushing Dolphins to the outer area of net

4

Boats allowing Dolphins to swim over net to the open sea

buy tuna only from fishing companies that guaranteed to supply "dolphin-safe" tuna (specially marked on tuna cans and available worldwide). The international consuming public made an impact as people looked for dolphin-safe tuna cans and boycotted tuna from companies that had the blood of dolphins on their hands.

Since the beginning of the 1990s, no seine fleet manages to work unnoticed and unsupervised for too long and every action of the tuna-seine fishermen is monitored by conservation groups.

Dolphins (and whales) are listed under the new European Union Directive, and special areas of conservation have been identified to protect the habitats of these and other marine mammals. Because of their wide distribution in the seas, oceans and rivers of this world, cetaceans are also protected under the Bonn Convention, an agreement concerned with species that travel widely through the territorial waters of various countries. Governments have accepted international agreements and have formulated domestic legislation. Some countries, however, need still to change their fishing and hunting policies in order to adapt to the international environmental awareness that seeks to protect our wildlife and ensure its well-being.

The Amazon river in Brazil

River dolphins: A special and endangered group

River dolphins constitute a special group that inhabit some of the major rivers of the world, namely, the Amazon in Brazil, the Ganges and Indus rivers in India, Pakistan and Bangladesh, the Irrawady in Myanmar (Burma), and the Yangtze in China. River dolphins belong to three or four related families that invaded freshwater habitats during the course of their evolution.

The one particular habitat on this earth that is continuously being destroyed, polluted and exploited is the rivers. As a direct consequence, all living creatures that live in them are showing alarming signs of decline, both in their numbers and in their general well-being.

The main threat to river dolphins is the destruction of their world. Rivers (and the seas and oceans for that matter) have become, in our "modern" times, a dumping ground for the waste products of industry. Pesticides, oils and heavy metals are all being drained off into the river and they either become part of the food chain of the animals inhabiting it or are simply swallowed by mistake.

The Amazon River dolphin (the bouto)

The Amazon River dolphin (the bouto) swims quite slowly as compared with other dolphins; it rolls to breathe on the surface and performs the occasional leap out of the water. Its eyes are small but they can still see in the muddy waters of the river.

Amazon River dolphins can be found in various river systems throughout South America and they have been observed to number between one and twenty dolphins in a group. A special problem these dolphins have to face is the flooding of the river. When this happens (not a rare event in tropical forests), they actually swim toward the banks of the river and into the flooded forests and stay there until the water level drops again. This puts them at risk of being caught in ponds and estuaries when the water recedes and of being cut off from the river, completely stranded.

One more problem – a much more serious one – the Amazon dolphin faces is the exploitation of its home. Since humans have begun to build dams on the river, the number of dolphins has started to decline alarmingly. It is not only the fact that they cannot roam freely anymore, but the reduction in their living space has had an immediate impact on their biology, behavior and reproduction.

The Ganges River dolphin (the Susu)

The Asiatic river dolphins include two species that are both named susu. One is the Ganges River dolphin, which inhabits the Ganges River in India and Bangladesh, and the other is the Indus River dolphin found in Pakistan. These two closely related species are highly developed. They have complex air sinuses in the skull that give their head a unique, bulbous appearance. These dolphins are virtually blind. They live in the muddy waters of the rivers and use their echolocation skills to locate and hunt their prey, in addition to probing the bottom of the river for fish and small creatures.

The susu are also going through a very difficult phase as their habitat is methodically destroyed. They are slow breeders and the reduction in available living space reduces their breeding rate even further. Most of the damage to the Indus and Ganges Rivers is being caused by damming, pollution and even hunting. Although hunting is illegal according to the legislations of the Indian, Bangladesh and Pakistani governments, it continues nevertheless. In 1998, reports estimated the populations of the Indus River dolphin and the Ganges River dolphin in Nepal to be 400 (split into small groups) and 40, respectively!

The Irrawady dolphin in Myanmar (Orcella brevirostris)

If there is one dolphin that has managed to escape human awareness and general knowledge, it is the Irrawady River dolphin in Myanmar (Burma). Some people are not even sure where the Irrawady River is. In fact, the Irrawady River runs from the north of Burma down to the south, where it joins the Andaman Sea (or the Bay of Bengal) – a distance of 2,000 km. The Irrawady dolphin is pale to dark-bluish gray in color and has a robust body, bulbous head and no distinct beak. They are around 60 cm long at birth and grow to a length of 2.2 meters.

They are slow swimmers and prefer the protected environments of warm and shallow estuaries or the inshore muddy waters of the more tropical areas.

Irrawady river dolphin

Although they mostly inhabit the Irrawady River, they have also been sighted in Thailand, Papua New Guinea and even northern Australia. The population of the Irawaddy dolphin in the Mekong river will be listed Critically Endangered In the year 2004 Red List. The same situation can be expected in the Ayeyarwady river in Myanmar (Burma).

The baiji (Lipotez vexillifer)
The dolphin of the Yangtze River in China

The vast country of the Chinese people is home to a wealth of endemic species, that is to say, animals (or plants) that live in no other place on the planet. One famous example is the panda, of course, which is a much-loved symbol of the Chinese bamboo forests. However, the baiji dolphin, also an endemic species, always lived in the Yangtze River (at 5,800 km, the longest river in China) quite anonymously, until world attention focused on it because of its new and unfortunate status as the most endangered dolphin species in the world.

The meaning of the name baiji in Chinese is the white flag dolphin and it was mentioned in ancient texts from as early as 200 BC.

The dolphin is equipped with a highly developed echolocation faculty in response to the very silty waters of the river (see Chapter 2 for further details).

The baiji, which can reach 2.1 meters in length, is not completely white, but more of a light to dark bluish gray on its back, fading to white on its belly. The dolphins once inhabited the whole river, but now they live only in the middle and lower reaches of it. Only an estimated 200 individuals remain in the Yangtze today.

Many different reasons have reduced it to this endangered state. These include intentional killing for the animal's skin and meat (though these are isolated cases), unintentional fishing, entanglement in fishing gear, collision with boats (the Yangtze boat traffic is among the busiest in the world), pollution of the river, over-fishing by the local fishermen, and most of all, the destruction of their habitat.

Dams and water barriers have blocked their free passage and have changed the distribution of fish schools. The Chinese government has launched a megalomanic dam project called the Three Gorges Dam, which is already under construction and will be finished around 2009. The dam will affect the lives of people and animals lives dramatically: when the river is flooded, millions of people will have to be relocated since the water level will be hundreds of meters higher and its natural course altered. Environmental organizations worldwide have tried to prevent the project, but to no avail.

However, there might still be hope for the baiji. The Chinese government is waging an educational campaign to make local fishermen aware of the dolphins in their waters and teach them alternative fishing methods. (1) The Baiji is now a formally "protected" animal under Chinese legislation and the intentional killing of a dolphin leads to severe penalties. (2) The Chinese government has allocated several protected areas for the dolphins. (3) Semi-natural environments are being developed so that the dolphins can live quietly. (4) A semi-captive breeding program is being designed to breed the baiji in conditions of semi-captivity and later release them into the wild. Such natural reserves can also help scientists in their efforts to study the dolphins (in non-intrusive ways), since studying them in the wild has proved to be a very difficult task.

Zhenjiang, a city on the lower reaches of the Yangtze River, is building a new nature reserve for the dolphins. The section of the Yangtze river that flows through the city of Zhenjiang constitutes one of the most important habitats for the white flag dolphin. The reserve will be half enclosed and less shipping traffic will pass through it as a result.

Some riverside towns have such breeding facilities within their boundaries and have adopted the baiji as their symbolic and honored pet animal. In the town of Tongling, a beautiful sculpture has been erected in honor of the dolphin (see photo on page 122). We can only hope and pray that this sculpture will never become a memorial to these rare, shy and graceful dolphins.

The Indus River dolphin

The Indus River in Pakistan is subdivided by huge concrete barrages that permanently divide dolphin populations. They are probably one of the causes that have contributed to the decline in the dolphin populations in the river by preventing potential breeding. Back in the 1990s, scientists agreed that the population of the Indus river dolphins is almost extinct, and these species received worldwide attention ever since.

However, good news recently arrived from the Indus River, where conservationists who are working to save the dolphins from extinction say that the population appears to be stabilizing in some areas, and as opposed to speculations made 10-20 years ago, they asses populations to number thousands/in the thousands. This is indicative of our lack of knowledge: it seems that different parts of the river have never been researched before and have begun to receive attention only quite recently. However, they caution that pollution and degradation of habitat are still a major threat and encourage the governments to employ urgent means to stop destruction of river and prevent dolphins' deteriorating conditions.

Chapter 8

Spontaneous swimming with dolphins

This chapter focuses on an interesting phenomenon that has been documented by humans worldwide since ancient times. To this day, it is still as mysterious and inexplicable as it has been for centuries, and is thus a source of fascination for laymen and scientists alike. This is the phenomenon of wild and lone dolphins that swim close to shore, approach humans and initiate communication with them on an entirely unconditioned basis. The words lone dolphins already inspire questions, since dolphins live and migrate in groups and have a highly developed system of communication (see Chapters 5 and 6 for further details). They depend on each other for food foraging and protection against predators (such as sharks), and are generally among the most social animals in existence. If this is the case, how does a dolphin find itself alone, separated from the rest of its group? The answer to this is still unknown. Of course, this solitary state is not always permanent. Frequently, it is temporary – it may be the result of the loss of the dolphin's companions, or it may be triggered by a need to find food elsewhere. Such a dolphin may eventually rejoin its group, never to return, or it might simply come to shore for short or long "visits". However, there are many cases in which a lone dolphin, a couple of dolphins or even a whole group (see Monkey Mia dolphins on page 132 for further details) stay close to shore, approaching and befriending humans for long and continuous periods of time, sometimes even for generations.

Sociability with humans evolves as a result of the dolphin's solitary circumstances and exposure to human activity. A large percentage of such encounters involves bottlenose dolphins, which, being coastal dolphins, part of whose natural habitat includes living close to the shoreline, are inevitably drawn to awareness of and mutual contact with humans.

Up till now, there have been recorded accounts of about seventy cases worldwide of solitary and sociable dolphins making contact with humans. This number might be much bigger, since there may be cases that have not become famous or publicized.

Another question regarding these encounters is whether the dolphins "need" to have this contact with people and are dependent on it.

Some answers have emerged from studies on solitary dolphins. First of all, it is not possible to generalize about the personality of these dolphins, the circumstances of their solitary state or the characteristics of the encounter. Each dolphin is unique in its personality, level of direct approach, shyness and length of visiting periods. Moreover, the dolphin's age is relevant. The younger a dolphin is when it first encounters humans, the more relaxed and accustomed to them it will be in the future. A great deal depends on past encounters with people: if a dolphin has had a bad experience with people, it will not re-initiate contact. Also, we must keep in mind that the first stages of such encounters may be coincidental and not necessarily intentional from the dolphin's point of view. A lone dolphin may be swimming close to a human habitat, preoccupied with catching fish and other activities, not in the least interested in interacting with humans, and at the moment of discovery by people, it might be regarded as a non-social dolphin. Later, it might become accustomed to human presence and activity and slowly but surely begin to show interest in humans, until it even initiates interaction and is not afraid or shy when swimmers approach it in the water.

Such encounters have been recorded since very early times. One of the oldest ones is described in a letter from Pliny the Young, written around 110 AD:

In the small town of Hippo on the north coast of Tunisia, a young boy used to live. The boy befriended a dolphin that had saved him from drowning. They used to meet every day and play for hours on end together. The dolphin let the boy ride him on his back. With time, the village people learned about this special friendship and gathered near the edge of the water to watch the amazing encounter. The rumors spread and many visitors, coming even from many miles afar, came to the village to see the wonder with their own very eyes. The town became very crowded and many locals changed their business into some kind of trade or service accommodating the crowds. However, as the number of visitors became yet greater, the town couldn't cater for all of them. They were short of accommodation, water, facilities and the like. Soon many arguments broke out between the locals and the harmony and stability that once characterized it were destroyed. Then, the elders decided it was high time to do something before it was too late and they killed the dolphin.

This very sad and disturbing event may really have taken place. Encounters between dolphins and humans have been known and witnessed in many places around the world. These encounters can be divided into two main types: the first and more frequent occurs when a few dolphins or an entire school of them follow ships and boats in the open seas and oceans. They sometimes accompany boats, bow-riding on the waves they create or just following from afar. The second type, which allows for more direct contact with dolphins, occurs when a lone dolphin – or sometimes many of them – approaches the shore and allows humans to touch it. We must bear in mind that it is the decision and desire of such free-ranging dolphins to come so close to the shore and approach humans. They are absolutely free to turn around and disappear within seconds into the expanses of the ocean.

However, sometimes the situation is not nearly as ideal. Wild dolphins that are resting or socializing among themselves close to the shoreline (see Chapter 6 for further details) may constantly be bothered by swimmers or worse still by speeding motorboats and jet-skiers. This in spite of the fact that it is obvious from the dolphins' behavior that at that very moment they would prefer to be left alone. Even when dolphins do want to make contact with people, there are always people who behave completely inappropriately toward them by not leaving them alone, chasing them and trying to catch hold of their flippers and fins and ride them. They also try to feed them completely unsuitable things that may be dangerous to their health. In the 1980s in Hawaii, for instance, spinner dolphins in Kealakekua Bay used to spend a lot of time with swimmers. However, as the word about the dolphins spread, pressure started to increase as more and more visitors came over, some of them with kayaks. According to a team of researchers in the area, the dolphins now choose to spend less time with the swimmers. When they do come, they stay for shorter periods, and only come for 75 percent of the number of days they used to in the past.

The one misconception people seem to have regarding dolphins is that dolphins always want them there with them and that they can never be unpleasant or aggressive toward people. The source of this misconception can be found in the rich, diverse and international lure of dolphins as well as in the myths concerning the strange contact dolphins have had with people and how they have always helped humans and communicated with them of their free will. Dolphins, however, just like any other animal or human being, can sometimes become agitated or show signs of stress, and the swimmers should be able to identify this and leave them alone. Unfortunately, this is usually not the case. Dolphins used to alter their behavior to accommodate their interaction with the swimmers, but the people were much less attentive to the dolphins' needs and less flexible when it came to responding to the changes necessary at that moment. People seem to have so many expectations and beliefs about dolphins that it is sometimes difficult for them to think

about them as wild animals. As a result, they mistreat them. In 2000, a group of Risso's dolphins arrived at the western shores of the Italian peninsula. The news of the dolphins' visit quickly spread through the local community and tourist hotels and many speedboats began to pull in, surrounding the dolphins completely. The people were so excited at seeing the dolphins and being in such close proximity to them that they did not realize that the dolphins were feeling quite distressed. As a result, the encounter, which had begun in a quiet and friendly way for the dolphins, became a stressful event for them. The moment a small gap appeared between some of the boats, the dolphins vanished like a shot. They disappeared the way they arrived and it is questionable whether they will ever visit again.

While this is not the case everywhere, it does happen, and everything must be done to educate people so as to prevent such occurrences. People should appreciate the fact that they can watch dolphins in the wild, in their own habitat.

Here are some accounts of encounters between people and dolphins from around the world.

Opo, New Zealand

One of the earliest and most famous of the records of a lone dolphin approaching humans in the sea describes the case of Opo. Opononi is a small township just inside the Hokianga Harbor, on the western side of the north island of New Zealand.

Early in 1955, the boat-owners of the Hokianga noticed a creature approaching the harbor. At first, they thought it was a shark because of its black fin, but later they noticed that it was following boats, which is a dolphin's unique behavior. They soon realized that it was indeed a dolphin. Before long, the whole area had heard about the friendly dolphin and began to look for it. The dolphin started to come closer to the boats, and gradually the locals discovered that it liked being scratched and petted. Then, the dolphin started to make the acquaintance of people in the water, although it was very cautious and always maintained a certain distance. The dolphin, a female, became known by the name of Opo. As time went by, she began to play games with people, tossing colorful balls in the air and rolling on her back to be stroked and scratched. Those who witnessed Opo and her behavior emphasized her playfulness. A common description of her was: "She was just like a dog, a real children's playmate." It was true that Opo was especially happy and amenable with children. She knew exactly which children were gentle and preferred to play with them. According to the records, the whole town loved Opo and became so attached to her that celebrations and holidays were revolved around her. People would take picnic hampers to the beach and stay there while the children played with her in the water. One day, Opo came too close to one of the boats in the harbor and was injured by its spinning propeller. The whole town agonized as Opo disappeared completely out of sight. Amazingly, she returned a few days later with clear signs of the injuries near her head.

She made a couple of leaps in the air, as if she wanted to show the people that she was all right. It looked as if she really wanted to reassure her friends.

Throughout the country, there was a feeling that over and above the protection afforded to Opo by the locals, the law should protect her in a formal way. Back in 1904 the government of New Zealand had already protected all Risso's dolphins:

"…it shall not be lawful for any person to take the fish or mammal of the species commonly known as Risso's Dolphin (Grampus griseus) in the waters of Cook Straits or of the bays, sounds and estuaries adjacent thereto."

And so, in order to extend the regulations and afford Opo the right protection, new regulations, known as the "Fisheries (dolphin protection) regulations", were formulated in the first week of March 1956. They were published in the New Zealand Gazette on March 8, 1956, and became law at midnight that night:

"…it shall not be lawful for any person to take or molest any dolphin in the Hokianga Harbor…"

That very day, Opo failed to arrive in the harbor according to her daily habit. The following Friday, four boats started to look for her in the vicinity of the bay. In the afternoon hours, an elderly Maori found her dead body. Opo was caught in a crevice between some rocks at Koutu Point, a few miles from the harbor. The tide had gone out and she had been trapped in a small pool, unable to release herself. When the news of her death spread through town, people felt genuine sadness, combined with shock and puzzlement. Why had she died like that? Many speculations were voiced (for instance, her echolocation abilities had been damaged, she had been trapped there accidentally or by some evil intent, she had committed suicide), but none was proved. To this day, no one knows how Opo, the beautiful friendly dolphin, ended her life in such a terrible way. The locals buried her and covered her grave with flowers.

Bottlenose dolphins in Monkey Mia, Western Australia

Monkey Mia, a small place on the shores of Shark Bay, on the eastern side of Denham Peninsula, Western Australia, began as a very quiet and relaxed fishing village. As the story goes (and there are many variations), one day in the 1960s, a local fisherwoman anchored her boat off the jetty at Shark Bay. Waking up in the middle of the night, she saw a lone dolphin splashing and blowing around the boat. She took a fish and threw it to the dolphin. Not too long afterwards, the dolphin started to take fish out of her hand. She called him Charlie and he became a favorite among fishermen and locals. Soon Charlie brought other dolphins into the bay and the bond with the locals was well established. Even after Charlie's death in the 1970s, dolphins continued to come and the contact developed further into a unique and beautiful friendship. Today, Monkey Mia is still a place of celebration: a celebration of the bonding between dolphins and humans, a celebration of two worlds meeting at one point. The only difference today is that the place is absolutely swarming with visitors, all eagerly traveling there for the rare opportunity of swimming and interacting with wild dolphins. The older locals, watching the tens of thousands of tourists, probably remember quieter days, but they seem happy to be the focus of attention for so many people from all corners of the world.

In 1986, special rangers were charged with the safety and welfare of the dolphins in the bay as a result of the increasing number of visitors. That year, the Australian government initiated a costly program to provide tourist facilities and information. Most importantly, it established a center to oversee the comings and goings of the masses of people in an orderly and supervised manner in order to ensure the dolphins' well-being. Laymen, visitors, writers and scientists alike are all amazed at the phenomenon, for it is the only place in the world in which a school of dolphins (as opposed to lone dolphins) have initiated contact with people and befriended humans in such a close and lasting way. In addition, the fact that the dolphins come close to the shore of the bay of their own free will in order to meet people is amazing, since most encounters with dolphins in the wild have occurred in the open seas – that is, in their world, not ours. Here, in order to experience intimate contact with people, they come so close to us that they sometimes even half-strand themselves on the shore.

There are about twenty Monkey Mia dolphins. Half of them come almost every day and some appear every now and then. Since the contact was established so many years ago, dolphins have been born during visits to the bay. As part of their "culture", the newborn babies have no doubt learned and experienced this contact from their mothers simply by watching it. For them, presumably, it is a normal and usual part of their lives.

With the increasing number of visitors, opportunists who saw the potential profits attempted to exploit the circumstances and turn the place into a "Dolphinarium" in which dolphins would jump, catch balls and the like. What that meant was actually placing the dolphins in a virtually captive situation. Fortunately, thanks to the efforts of the unofficial guardians of the dolphins, Wilf and Hazel Mason, these attempts were thwarted and strict regulations were formulated. Visitors were instructed not to initiate any games with the dolphins, not to ride on their backs, not to teach them any tricks, and so on. The most important requests, however, concerned the issue of feeding. As a result of ignorance, people offered the dolphins many kinds of foods that were absolutely unsuitable. Not only that – the wrong food could even kill them. We are all familiar with stories of visitors who feed animals in zoos the strangest things, actually causing them to become ill or even worse. It was no different here, but it seems that all the visitors have gradually learned how to behave with the dolphins: simply be there with them and greet their approach with nothing more than love. The place is what it really should be – a natural, relaxed, unconditioned meeting point between dolphins and humans, in which both sides enjoy each other. People coming to Monkey Mia should be grateful and thankful for this wonderful encounter as it is, without trying to abuse and exploit it, as unfortunately happens so often and so easily in numerous places around the planet. Let's hope that in the future, the current harmony that exists between humans and dolphins in Monkey Mia will not be destroyed, so that in the future it will still be possible for humans to experience the gift of interspecies communication.

Holly – Sinai, Egypt

In the early 1990s, people began to hear about a lone dolphin that interacted with the Bedouins in Sinai, or to be more precise, the Bedouin village of Nuweiba M'zeina. The fishermen of Sinai are famous for their diving capabilities, diving deep into the water without any masks or snorkeling equipment. They also suffer from hereditary deafness and are considered to be of lower social status for that reason. The fishermen say that the dolphin began to approach the shoreline one day, remaining close for a while and then disappearing again. The Bedouins went into the water with the dolphin and swam with it, sometimes for a long time.

As it turned out later, it was an adult female bottlenose dolphin. She was eventually given the name "Holly".

The Bedouins tried to touch Holly, but she did not let them. She allowed them to approach her and swim around her, all the while setting her limits clearly. Slowly, however, as she built up confidence and trust regarding her new friends, she permitted more and more contact. Holly seemed to form a special bond with one of the fishermen, a young deaf-mute Bedouin called Abd'allah. Gradually, the word spread, and more and more people came to the village in the hope of swimming with Holly. A real tourist venture flourished in the village, with people coming from far and wide and paying for swimming with Holly, renting snorkeling equipment and bungalows, and so on. The extent of the effect Holly has had on the Bedouins is amazing. A small and inconspicuous fishing village has become a real tourist attraction.

Unfortunately, some people abused the situation, harassing Holly and trying to grab her flippers and tail. However, she knew how to handle these swimmers and she issued warnings before teaching them a lesson… She would bite them gently or slap her tail if they demanded too much of her or were too pushy and aggressive.

Holly became pregnant three times between 1995 and 2000 and gave birth to two male calves and one female. Unfortunately, both male calves died. The theory as to the cause of death is related to the fact that

Holly raised them both among humans rather than among dolphins, and, as a result, they lacked the correct social context and vital communication needs.

When her third calf was born, Holly changed her behavior. She started to be much more protective of her calf and prevented her from encountering humans. As of 2000, Holly ceased coming to the village on a daily basis.

Since the pressure from swimmers sometimes becomes too much for her, Holly prefers to swim to other, quieter beaches.

Hopefully, Holly will be able to combine her solitary life with her special relationships with humans and succeed in raising her calf in an undisturbed and peaceful atmosphere in the future. While her well-being depends on the Bedouins of M'zeina village, it also seems that Holly is very intelligent and knows what is best for her. Her flexibility and adaptability with regard to the changing circumstances is a proof of her intelligence and free spirit.

Dusky, Ireland

Dusky, a lone dolphin, approached the area of West Clare, just south of Ballyvaughan and north of Doolin. Derreen is a small unmarked town just south of the small village of Fanore, famous for its sandy beaches.

Dusky made her first appearance in July 2000. Apparently, she had been hanging around Doolin for several months, possibly ranging over a gradually smaller area and becoming increasingly loyal to this one site near "the jump". Some people claim that she had been present in the same spot the previous summer, but there is no real proof of that. It is good when the first people to encounter a lone dolphin are people who understand and respect animals, and that was the case here. As a result, mutual trust began to form. The word spread through the surfing community in nearby Lahinch. Again, these were people (nearly all young men) who were used to the water and respectful toward its wildlife.

It is fortunate that there is no flat land to establish a caravan park, and although there are many new bungalows here, the general atmosphere is quiet and unspoiled by tourists. Frequently, what determines a good spot for "spontaneous swimming with dolphins" spot is the balance between people's attraction to the dolphins, which is understandable, and their respect for the dolphins' need for tranquillity as well.

It is peculiar that Dusty chose this particular location, since, as opposed to other shorelines approached by dolphins , there is no estuary, harbor or caves around here. The shoreline within the dolphin's adopted range is a rocky section of a wide sweeping bay, and is scarcely interrupted by a small concrete slipway at a point where the sea comes within 50 meters of the road. According to eyewitnesses, the moment people enter the water, Dusty suddenly appears out of nowhere. The seabed immediately by the shore is rich in kelp and other seaweed as well as in marine life. Luckily, the encounter between Dusty and people in Ireland has so far been peaceful and balanced. Let's hope it remains this way.

Mikura Island, Japan

Mikura Island is a dormant volcanic island and the shore near it ranges between five and twenty meters in width. Bottlenose dolphins approach the shore and travel both inshore and offshore. Programs for watching and swimming with dolphins there began only in 1994, and they are a huge success. The numbers of visitors are increasing steadily and regulations are in the process of being drawn up by the Fishermen's Cooperation Association in order to prevent the hoards of tourists from hurting the dolphins.

Chapter 9

Cooperation between fishermen and dolphins

In addition to current accounts of the cooperation between dolphins and fishermen as a result of the dolphins' free will and initiative, we have historical accounts of such collaboration in the past.

In the Mediterranean, Aelian and Apostolides described fishing by torchlight, according to which the fish, attracted by the lights, begin to gather and the dolphins appear in order to drive them into the fishermen's nets.

Similar methods were employed in New Zealand in the 19th century. On the Queensland coast, the natives of Moreton Bay would catch mullet with the assistance of dolphins. They spread their nets close to the shoreline and waited for a school of fish to appear. When they saw them, they banged their spears on the water and made special splashing noises that were heard by the dolphins. The latter then swam close by and drove the fish into the nets. Witnesses wrote that it was evident that an understanding existed between the dolphins and the natives. Each village had its own guardian dolphin, and the remarkable thing about the dolphins was their complete and utter lack of fear. According to the elderly people in New

Zealand, this kind of cooperation has existed for many generations. Among the fishermen themselves, it is difficult to find someone who remembers a different fishing method.

The pink Amazon River dolphin, the bouto, which inhabits the Amazon River of Brazil (see Chapter 3 for further details), is another species that assists fishermen. While paddling, the fishermen tap on the side of their canoes with their oars and whistle a peculiar-sounding tune. Immediately afterwards, a dolphin can be seen approaching and chasing the fish toward the canoe.

In the town of Laguna in Brazil, a very special type of cooperation exists between fishermen and dolphins. The fishermen gather on the beaches and start spreading their nets in order to catch mullet. Each fisherman has a nylon throw net with weights on its edges. They all stand on the sand with their nets ready. Dolphins gather in front of the men, facing the sea, floating slowly and waiting. Suddenly, the dolphins dive and in a few seconds are seen traveling at full speed toward the nets. On cue, the fishermen stand alert and grasp their nets firmly. The dolphins then come to an abrupt halt and dive out of the reach of the nets, performing a very special surging roll. The nets are suddenly filled with thousands of fish that were driven into them by the dolphins. The prize the dolphins get for this helpful cooperation with the fishermen is food. This is because the schools of fish get into a state of genuine panic. Some of them are caught inside the nets and some are free, and by the time they manage to reorganize themselves, they are completely disoriented. While this is happening, it is much easier for the dolphins to catch them than if they were one huge school. The rewards of this fascinating cooperation between fishermen and dolphins, which dates back hundreds of years, are great for both sides.

Fishermen along the coasts of Florida call dolphin and sharks the dogs and cats of the sea and they recount many tales of battles between them.

In Burma, the Irrawady river dolphins help the fishermen while fishing. The fishermen go out in their boats and start rowing with the oars. Then, after a while, they take a piece of wood (made specially for

**A fisherman with a dolphin in the
Irrawady river.**

that purpose) and start knocking on the side of the boats with it. They do not just knock on the boats – they produce a special drumming sound in a certain rhythm. The dolphins hear the sounds and slowly but surely approach. They start herding fish into the fishermen's nets. This is another example of wonderful cooperative behavior between dolphins and humans that has existed for hundreds of years and can still be witnessed in Burma today.

Chapter 10

Dolphins in display, therapy and research

Today, taking the family for a visit to the local "Dolphinarium" or "Oceanarium" (whether in one's own country or abroad) is still a very exciting experience, especially for children. In the past, however – only 30 or 40 years ago – that was not the case, and the opportunities to do so were very limited as compared to now.

The question of whether we should set up places in which dolphins are kept in captivity is still fraught with controversy. People may justifiably ask whether we have the right to confine these animals physically and train them to do all kinds of tricks and jumps for our own selfish enjoyment. However, if we do decide to establish such places, we should plan them in the best possible manner in order to ensure that the dolphins do not suffer in any way and that their well-being is a top priority in the list of guidelines for such a business.

The dispute over dolphinaria and oceanaria is characterized by many different opinions – each strongly convinced of its validity, of course. One opinion states that we actually need such public places in which we can watch dolphins, since there is very little chance that most people in the world will go on long expeditions to look for wild dolphins or whales (with the exception of local communities that are lucky enough to live near dolphins' habitat. Unfortunately, it is sometimes the locals themselves who take the dolphins for granted and mistreat them). Furthermore, if we want to educate people with regard to environmental awareness and teach them how important it is to preserve and protect wild animals, then dolphinaria contribute positively to the cause. There is no doubt that watching dolphins in such entertaining facilities has an impact on people's attitude and feelings toward them. Once they are aware of dolphins' intelligence and grace, there is a better chance that they will care more, and they will not be oblivious to the issue of dolphin conservation in the wild in the future. On the other hand, it is often said that watching marine mammals in captivity is also quite degrading as far as their grace and freedom are concerned.

Another opinion states that keeping dolphins in captivity for people to visit, swim with and watch, without training them to do displays, serves the same purpose as a zoo, and that we actually need to have them in order to further people's knowledge with regard to marine mammals.

One case that proves this line of argument (that is, that dolphinaria are actually important) involves the Orcas in Seymour Narrows, located between Vancouver and British Columbia. Back in the 1960s, the Orcas living in Seymour Narrow were considered to be very dangerous predators that posed serious competition to fishermen. In response to local public demand, the US Federal Department had serious plans to reduce the number of local Orcas by killing them with machine guns. However, in 1964-5, a few Orcas were captured and kept alive in captivity. This aroused tremendous interest and attracted crowds of visitors. Later still, a new shipping line began to operate cruises to watch the Orcas in the wild. With the new awareness of and the growing affection toward these magnificent animals as well as the elimination of the psychological fear people felt for them, a new attitude developed among the public. This eventually led to the formulation of new legal regulations for the protection and conservation of Orcas in the region.

The opposing opinion negates the positive value of dolphinaria. According to this opinion, if we want education and conservation, dolphins in captivity do not contribute to that cause at all, since it actually teaches people that dolphins are not strongly attached to their natural habitat, but can in fact be very happy and content in captivity. In addition, it might convey a false message that just as the dolphins in captivity interact and swim with people, the same rules must apply in nature as well. Logically, this would mean that people have the right to initiate contact with the dolphins instead of waiting for the dolphins to allow people to interact with them in their own habitat. Some say that watching dolphins in captivity (especially in places where they also perform) teaches people, in effect, to disrespect dolphins. Sadly enough, perceiving marine mammals as "something to play with in the water" is possible in the wild as well.

Photo: Galit Amiel. Dolphin Reef, Eilat, Israel.
Website: www.dolphinreef.co.il

The history of training facilities for displays is fairly brief. It started in the 1870s, when five belugas were put on display in England. In 1913, bottlenose dolphins and harbor porpoises were kept in an aquarium in New York.

In the 1930s, The Marine Biological Association of the United Kingdom in Plymouth displayed animals that had been rescued from a live stranding. In 1938, Marine Studios in Florida started to shoot underwater footage of dolphins in a tank. As training began, crowds gathered to watch, and it was clear to the company that they found it fascinating. This was the first place and the first time that people could watch the dolphins as they trained, played, jumped and interacted with each other. The first dolphin trainer at Marine Studios was Adolph Frohn, who trained a dolphin by the name of Flippy. In 1976, there were 365 cetaceans on display in the U.S. By 1984, the number had risen to 1,341 marine mammals. In 1979, 18 percent of all bottlenose dolphins in the U.S. had been born in captivity. By 1983, however, all captive dolphins were already second-generation, that is, they had all been born in captivity.

After keeping a dolphin in captivity for a long time, it is not simple to release it back to the wild. Dolphins become accustomed to the food they have been feeding on, namely, dead fish. There have been accounts of dolphins refusing to eat live fish when these were offered to them, which is a sign of how accustomed they have become to the conditions imposed upon them. In addition, in the case of dolphins returning to the open waters and trying to rejoin groups of wild dolphins, there is no guarantee that the group will give them a warm welcome. The males of the new group might even attack the intruding newcomers, from fear that they the new males will take over the group (i.e., the males of the group might lose their dominant position to the new comers). Captive dolphins that are released to the wild have sometimes been seen to go back and try to return to their captive home, to which they apparently became so accustomed.

At a time when extensive parts of the earth are in the process of being destroyed, marine mammals have not escaped the impact, and many species are on the verge of extinction. In the same way that many other species are kept in zoos, safaris and zoological parks around the world in order to preserve them before they disappear altogether, so perhaps dolphinaria can serve that purpose as well. However, people must consider how to run them and whether it is really necessary that dolphins be made to perform in front of the public in these facilities.

Not all dolphins kept in captivity are there for display (either swimming programs or performances). Some facilities have been founded for the purpose of research, since free-ranging dolphins are so difficult to research in the wild (see Chapter 6 for further details). Researching dolphins in captivity focuses on general behavior, recording and analyzing vocal communication and studying communication in general among the group members, mother-calf communication and behavior, intelligence, social interactions, and so on.

Training

The primary purpose of training dolphins was to display them to the public as a business venture. However, it has created a by-product: the understanding and realization of how intelligent dolphins are and how impressive their learning capability is, as well as their communication skills among themselves and with their trainers. Their ability to perform new and novel behavioral tasks amazed trainers back in the 1960s.

As already mentioned in chapter on Intelligence, dolphins also learn through a process of imitating. Further more, they have an ability to imitate the use of tools. . Watching humans using tools such as cleaning devices or playing objects, the dolphins in the tank were observed making the same movement, even if they could not use the tool itself. In experiments conducted at the Kewalo Basin Marine Mammal Laboratory in Hawaii, one dolphin was given a command to perform, while another one watched the first dolphin performing, but could not see the command itself. The second one was then asked to perform what the first one was doing. It did so. They were also taught to perform in synchrony, a task requiring a high level of intelligence, awareness of the other dolphin's performance and highly complex communication skills.

Dolphins are also able to imitate sounds. In one experiment, dolphins were taught to imitate computer-generated sounds that were not in their repertoire. The dolphins were not only able to do that – they even began to play around with the loudness of the sounds. Dolphins were taught to associate sounds with objects and later to produce the sound when the object was displayed. They "passed" these tests successfully. Scientists are not certain whether the ability to mimic sounds is a natural skill, that is to say, whether dolphins mimic each other's sounds in nature.

Research

One of the pioneers in the field of researching dolphins in captivity back in the 1960s was Dr. John Lilly, who died in 2001. John Lilly was a very controversial scientist because he employed methods that were (at the time) very innovative and daring. His research got off to a bad start as a result of a lack of experience – some of his dolphins died following his experiments. He also conducted highly intrusive experiments that were questioned from the ethical point of view (for instance, connecting electrodes to the dolphin's brain or using LSD). His work exerted a tremendous influence not only on other researchers, but also on people worldwide as he declared dolphins to be highly developed beings and an "extraterrestrial intelligence on earth" and dedicated his life to proving it. He called for interspecies communication between dolphins and humans (an opinion that, needless to say, did not arouse too much scientific sympathy from colleagues in the academic world).

Photo: Galit Amiel. Dolphin Reef, Eilat, Israel. Website: www.dolphinreef.co.il

Dr. Lilly studied the intelligence of dolphins and their communication with humans. He used a variety of creative and controversial experiments, the last series of which included sharing life with the dolphins in a regular house, half of which was in the water and half "normal" (that is, with floors, chairs, tables, and so on). The idea was to create an environment that consisted of the two distinct worlds of people and dolphins, and live together just like roommates. The dolphins were free to come to John and his wife Toni's half of the house (their half was a pool and the water's edge was in the middle of John and Toni's room) whenever they wanted and watch how John and Toni lived (something that, as John Lilly said, dolphins never had a chance to see, although we see their world all the time), and John and Toni could watch and interact with the dolphins whenever they wanted.

During the last years of his life, and due to Toni's deteriorating health, they decided to release the two captive dolphins that had been with them for years. Thus, Joe and Rosie were released to the wild and were documented by the National Geographic Society.

There is no doubt that the fact that John Lilly, a serious scientist, perceived dolphins to be an "extraterrestrial intelligence" and called for an interspecies interaction with them, significantly enhanced the myth that already surrounded them. He took mythology into the laboratory and took science out to people's everyday lives. In his last years, Dr. Lilly made a worldwide appeal to meet dolphins as equals and listen to what they have to say to us, since they are the most intelligent creatures on earth or at least equal to humans. He called for the creation of a Cetacean Nation, an organization

Photo: Galit Amiel. Dolphin Reef, Eilat, Israel.

that would establish understanding between humans and dolphins, be an active part of the United Nations,

Website: www.dolphinreef.co.il

and take part in the organization's decisions as the representative of the Cetacean World (see Appendix on Cetacean Nation).

Since John Lilly's days, many experiments seeking to understand dolphins' intelligence better have been conducted in various laboratories worldwide. In the wild, it is an entirely different matter. While it is actually a very difficult task to research dolphins in the wild, some passionate researchers back in the 1970s started investigating wild dolphins and contributed to our present knowledge in an unparalleled way. To begin with, one needs to observe a group of dolphins from a distance that permits one to recognize the individuals and watch them playing, mating, fighting and feeding. Then, in order to come up with results that provide a better understanding of their social bonding and behavior, it is necessary to observe the same group again and again over a long period of time, preferably for many years. With all the difficulties involved in investigating free-ranging dolphins, social behavior is one specific area that cannot be explored without such observations. Obviously, a group of dolphins in captivity or even semi-captivity does not exhibit the same social patterns or enjoy the same social flexibility as it does in the wild. To make things even more complicated, modern science has proved that one cannot rely on observations only. In order to determine the exact blood relations between individuals, scientists need DNA, which can be extracted from DNA-containing tissue such as the dolphin's skin

Below are the different methods employed to research wild dolphins, including modern techniques that help scientists gather information in very sophisticated ways:

Patiently observing the group of animals for long periods of time, sometimes even years, in order to understand distribution, family ties, seasonal changes, social, sexual and other kinds of behaviors, etc.

Radio transmitters and hydrophones for detecting and recording dolphin sounds.

Underwater video cameras.

A submarine tracking system that started in the US navy.

Photo identification (photo-ID): This method was developed in the 1970s and changed the face of dolphin and whale research forever. It was used with the purpose of identifying individual dolphins and whales in the wild, so that over years of observations, scientists can tell exactly which dolphins they are watching and which dolphins interact with which, and study their social lives and life span. In populations that have been studied using this method, identification began immediately with the birth of a baby, which meant that it was possible to follow an individual dolphin or whale for years, through its childhood, adolescence and adulthood. The key to identifying dolphins is the fact that each dolphin – even though to the inexperienced eye it resembles its companions – has special and unique markings that differentiate it from the rest of the group. These markings include size, the shape of the whole body, the shape of the dorsal fin, marks and scars on the skin, and so on. Each dolphin was photographed and each photograph was then studied carefully to locate those key markings. Over time, scientists could tell by sight which dolphins they were seeing in real time.

Satellite telemetry: One of the most difficult tasks in the study of cetaceans in the wild is keeping track of them for long distances. The research of the distribution of whales and dolphins and their ecology and migration habits depends on our knowledge of their whereabouts. For that purpose, a new and sophisticated technique was recently invented and employed successfully. Scientists fire a small, battery-powered transmitter into the blubber layer (the thick layer of fat under dolphins and whales' skin that evolved as insulation against the cold water). This does not hurt the dolphin or cause it any discomfort. The transmitter sends signals to the satellite, which sends the information back to stations on earth. The satellite thus keeps track of the dolphins wherever they travel on earth, and in addition transmits valuable information concerning their movements, swimming patterns, heart rate, water temperature, and so on. Another fantastic advantage of this method is that the researchers themselves can sit hundreds or thousands of kilometers away from the dolphins and receive the data straight into their computers.

DNA fingerprint: Taking a small sample of a whale or a dolphin's skin and examining its DNA can provide a great deal of information about their genetics – how individuals are related to each other, how many of the young have the same father, and other intriguing questions. The DNA fingerprint method is very valuable in researching wild dolphins and whales in particular. Not only can the relationships between the different members of the group be found, but also what species a particular dolphin belongs to in case of difficulty in identifying one or a group of dolphins in the wild.

Dolphins in the military

Ever since Hannibal of Carthage crossed the Alps with the help of elephants, or the Burmese and Thai people used elephants, not to mention horses, in their wars, animals have been used in human warfare. Dolphins played specific roles in maritime combat and are still used in various centers in the world, such as the U.S. and Russia.

As recently as the Gulf War, dolphins were used by the U.S. Navy to replace anti-mine systems in the Persian Gulf. The mines in the waterways are larger than land mines and can also float freely in the water. Dolphins are capable of detecting explosives and frogmen since their natural sonar system is much more effective than man-made machines and the most sophisticated equipment. Their echolocation system helps them detect the mines, which are made of metal. Dolphins served in the Iraq war instead of sea lions, which were used to detect hazards in shallow waters. The dolphins were trained to track the mines and mark them with floating buoys. Once they marked the mines, navy divers came to the spot and detonated them after the dolphins had been removed from the area.

This was not the first time dolphins were used in military service of that kind and, unfortunately, it will probably not be the last. Dolphins have been trained to locate mines, to put bombs on ships and to perform other such missions since the early 1970s. It seems that the Russians were the first to identify their potential in the navy's military missions. The Russian scientists, by the way, were also pioneers in dolphin research in general and in their training in particular. It was the Russians, for example, that first discovered the dolphins' fascinating sleep patterns (which utilize their brain hemispheres alternatively) by attaching electrodes to their heads (see Chapter 4 for further details).

The U.S. navy has been using dolphins for thirty years now, ever since the Vietnam War. Sometimes, small cameras are attached to the dolphins' dorsal fins in order to help divers identify the type and size of mines. There are certainly other ways for the navy to detect mines, such as mine-sweeping vessels or helicopters that detect mines from the air.

Many animal welfare organizations worldwide are concerned about recruiting innocent animals for such military missions and call for a more ethical treatment of dolphins. According to them, "War is a human endeavor and innocent animals should not be put in harm's way because of our stupid behavior. Dolphins treat the location of mines as a game, but they do not realize what will happen in the event of a single failure."

Dolphins in therapy

It is interesting to note the many different types of therapy that have flourished in the modern world during the past couple of decades. The concept of therapy is changing and people realize that there are many ways in which they can foster their well-being and cope with their psychological, mental and emotional needs and difficulties. Along with drama, music, literature, dance and art therapy, animal therapy has gained much attention lately among the general public and among experts in the field of psychology. It is

now becoming an increasingly accepted method of treatment for people who used to be treated with traditional therapy and psychiatric means only (for instance, mental patients, children with special needs, the elderly, trauma victims, autistic children, children who have suffered abuse, and many more). The world is now ready to face the challenge posed by this new approach.

It is interesting to note, however, that animal therapy is not a new phenomenon. The ancient Greeks were familiar with it and expressed their opinion that physical contact with animals had a mental and emotional impact on people. The first written document to be found so far regarding the involvement of animals in therapy comes from Yorkshire, U.K. In 1792, pet animals were introduced into a mental institution in order to reduce the use of drugs and psychiatric medicines. The patients were encouraged to take care of the animals, to feed them and to give them attention, love and care – a process that had positive consequences for their emotional well-being. This kind of therapy has served as a model to this very day and is being introduced into more and more institutions.

Animal therapy has frequently succeeded with special populations that experience acute difficulty in developing contact and communication with other people. The aim is to help these people build a bridge to society by forming contacts with pet animals. This would enable them to develop their trust in the animals and receive the latter's trust and unconditional love in return.

In the framework and concept of animal therapy, not all animals are suitable (because of size, temperament, personality, appearance, external features, potential to make contact with humans, and so on), but quite a few species have already been introduced. Among others we have horses (therapy through riding), mice, cats, dogs, birds, rabbits, and, of course, dolphins.

Dolphins seem to be excellent companions in therapy because of their special qualities that have become almost legendary. These include the constant and welcoming "smile" on their faces, their famous affinity for people, their desire to make contact with people (even in the wild, which has been documented worldwide since ancient times), their special friendliness with people, their love of touch, the sounds they produce, which have been found to have a calming affect on people, their intelligent curiosity and the water in which they live, which is a very relaxing and beneficial medium (floating in the water creates a primal "womb" sensation).

People suffering from different kinds of mental problems are trying dolphin therapy (called "Dolphin Assisted Therapy" or DAT) these days. Children with special needs, autistic children, children who suffer from slow development, blind and deaf children and adults, children who suffer from abuse and traumas, handicapped children and adults, children suffering from Attention Deficiency Disorder, and others can all benefit from DAT.

In dolphin therapy, the patient gets into the water with one or two dolphin dolphins. From that moment on, therapists are divided as to how and what should follow. Some believe that the patient and the dolphins should be given specific tasks for which they will both be rewarded. Others believe that the dolphins themselves are the therapists and what takes place in the water is completely up to the dolphin and the patient: a spontaneous meeting with many possible developments and consequences.

What one often hears from people who have been through or witnessed such therapy is how "emotionally intelligent" the dolphins seem to be, that is to say, how adaptable and flexible they are with regard to people's different needs and how they manage to react differently to each and every patient, according to his or her specific problem. They seem to be attentive to and aware of the patient's difficulties. However, the problem is whether this interpretation is our own emotional reaction to the encounter or a true description of a genuine and amazing phenomenon. Another criticism that has been voiced concerning therapy with dolphins (or any other animal therapy, for that matter) is the difficulty in scientifically assessing and evaluating the benefits of this kind of therapy for the patients.

The conceptual foundations of DAT are generally believed to have started in 1971 during an encounter between a group of dolphins and the mentally retarded brother of Dr. B. Smith, a famous anthropologist. She began to notice changes in her brother's behavior and realized the potential of such encounters in therapeutic applications. Since that day, DAT has become a worldwide industry and an increasingly popular field of scientific investigation. Many countries are currently studying and applying DAT, including Israel, the U.K., Japan, Australia and the U.S.

The early development of DAT focused on the dolphins' ability to motivate behavioral and cognitive changes in children. Captive dolphins were used as stimuli to create responses and positive learning and enthusiasm. The children's desire to interact with dolphins and be with them in the water was accepted as the underlying concept for initiating response and behavioral change in them. Swimming with dolphins and feeding and petting them were indeed sufficient to motivate disabled children to learn and communicate. There is no doubt that the growing interest and New Age beliefs in dolphins and their powers has engendered an intense demand for DAT programs and made it a very sought-after therapy plan in the world today.

DAT is currently helping a wide range of disabilities. Here is a partial list: Cerebral palsy, autism, spinal and spinal cord injuries, strokes, cancer, post traumatic stress, retardation, blindness, deafness and muteness, chronic depression, anorexia, Attention Deficiency Disorder, Down's syndrome, muscular dystrophy, dyslexia and others.

What people often tend to forget are the dolphins themselves. They are wild animals and are used to their natural environment. Some programs seem to think that the dolphins are there only to help humans. (The result of having to be present all the time and responsive to the patients is the loss of their freedom.) In consequence, various organizations claim that therapy does not justify keeping dolphins in pools. Another major difficulty is scientifically assessing the therapeutic effect of DAT, since it would be necessary to eliminate other factors that might exert a positive influence on the patient (for instance, the relaxing effect of the water, improved self-esteem, heightened sensory perceptions and so on) in order to evaluate and understand the direct positive influence dolphins exert on patients.

In addition, the potential to exploit dolphins and humans that accompanies the growing interest and demand for DAT is a major concern. People would be willing to do a great deal and pay a lot of money for the rare opportunity of attaining joy and happiness with dolphins in the water and for the hope that the experience will have positive effects or even bring about a total cure. (This refers to patients who might have lost all other hope with regard to traditional medical methods.) Specific laws, regulations and standards must be laid down for DAT (and any alternative therapy for that matter) in order to prevent the exploitation of dolphins and humans in that field.

There are people who believe that dolphins have the ability to perform distance healing! This means that it is not necessary to swim with them, because their power reaches the people watching them on TV, reading about them in books and listening to music inspired by them. One person who strongly believes in that theory and has revolutionized the concept of dolphins' healing powers is Dr. Horace Dobbs. According to his personal story, one day during the 1970s, while on vacation in the Irish Sea off the Isle of Man, he formed a special relationship with a dolphin named Donald. He claimed that this experience changed his life completely, and he went on to produce a documentary film for the BBC. Surprisingly, after the film was broadcast, the BBC received letters from viewers who suffered from depression. They reported that the film had lifted their spirits, and some seriously chronically depressed patients attested to the fact that the film had brought some happiness into their lives. What followed was a lifelong quest into dolphins' healing powers and the development of a whole range of different methods that Dobbs believed could promote the mental and emotional well-being of people. (An example is a CD called Dolphin Dreamtime, which is used as a tool in psychiatric patients and institutions.) In addition, he placed paintings of dolphins in hospitals and written books about an imaginary dolphin called Dilo. Both projects had such a positive effect on children (whether healthy or sick in hospital) that since then, a full research program called the "Dolphin Education Research Project" has been established, its purpose being to provide scientific evidence and data to support the introduction of dolphin-related stories, art and education into schools and other institutions and to help children attain their full potential.

As an example of how powerful such experiences can be and their influence on people, it is interesting to hear what Princess Irene of Holland, who recommends swimming with dolphins as a tool for self-explo-

Photo: Galit Amiel.
Dolphin Reef, Eilat, Israel.
Website: www.dolphinreef.co.il

ration and mental balance, has to say. She has written a successful book entitled Dialogue with Nature: A Way to a New Equilibrium. It it, she describes her constant communion with animals, plants and various metaphysical phenomena. She also describes her struggle to come to terms with her life and make her existence worthwhile. She mentions how dolphins have been of enormous help to her: once when she was depressed, she read about a woman in Hawaii who organized therapeutic sessions with dolphins. She went there and swam with the dolphins, and describes their amazing sensuality. She writes: "One morning, I shamelessly told everything about myself to a large male dolphin. I asked him whether I should write about it. He told me. 'You will get everything, everything.' And then he gave a shower of bubbles all over me... then, that night, I chose [the path) for my life and the dolphins showed me the way."

It was recently reported that people who swam with dolphins experienced a decrease in anxiety. Nicola Webb, Ph.D., examined psychological and physiological well-being in individuals who swam with captive dolphins in Western Australia. She found that people who swam with dolphins experienced a greater sense of well-being and significantly lower anxiety levels as compared to swimmers who did not swim with dolphins at all. In this context, it is worth mentioning that in patients suffering from high blood pressure and high anxiety levels, both levels immediately decreased and an immediate effect of well-being was felt when they were given furry animals such as cats and rabbits to hold and caress. Of course, further experiments are required to validate these findings.

Chapter 11

Dolphins in ancient myths, literature and art

Man has always been interested in the living creatures around him. This interest may have begun as a result of fear and the need to defend himself, or as a result of basic hunger, respect or even curiosity. With the passage of time and the evolution of cultures, the human psyche increasingly perceived animals as sacred symbols of strength, potency, wisdom or any other quality that attracts the human heart. Among the many species that captured the attention and inspired the respect of various cultures, dolphins are definitely one of the most popular. They continue to evoke curiosity and awe and to be perceived as mysterious creatures to this very day. Indeed, the history of the dolphin in human historiography is a fascinating one. Dolphins became an important theme in Creation myths, characters in literature, and important, meaningful motifs in works of art. Archeological findings in France reveal that as early as 14,000 BC, dolphins, which were sacred animals, were involved in fertility rites. The writings of classical scholars such as Plutarch and Herodotus, the poets Pindar and Oppian, and the naturalist Aristotle provide realistic descriptions of encounters with dolphins, men being rescued by dolphins, cooperation with fishermen and amazing stories of friendships between dolphins and people. In Cyprus, dolphins are frequently depicted on late Hellenic vases, amphorae, engravings and stucco floors. Orcas have been the subject of many different art forms, both in indigenous cultures and in contemporary art. In northern Norway, very ancient drawings of orcas, estimated to be 7,000 years old, have been discovered. In Peru, the Nazca people built temples in honor of the spirits of killer whales. In the Icelandic culture, as opposed to the Native Americans and South America peoples, killer whales were perceived as "evil creatures" that attacked fishermen and sank their boats

Dolphins have been depicted in various works of art, not only in indigenous ones. Indeed, famous artists such as Raphael chose to depict them in their paintings, such as in his Galatea on the right:

Raphael's Galatea; 16th Century

Mediterranean lore

The ancient Greeks and subsequently the Romans considered the dolphins to be special. They lived close to the sea, of course, and that played a significant role in their lives. However, there are many civilizations other that live close to water (in fact, most of the great civilizations of the world started to evolve on the banks of major rivers such as the Ganges, Irrawady, Yangtze, Amazon, Nile and so on). Thus, their physical location per se cannot account for the Greeks' great fascination with dolphins. Below is the Greek myth regarding the creation of the dolphins:

Dionysos, the god of wine (later called Bacchus by the Romans), engaged a boat service to take him from the island of Ikaria to the island of Naxos. The sailors, however, were a gang of pirates who, unaware that they were actually conveying a god on their vessel, decided to abduct him. They sailed past Naxos and made their way toward Asia with the intention of selling him as a slave. When Dionysos realized what was happening, he summoned up his special magical powers, changed the oars into snakes and filled the ship with vine and ivy and the sound of flutes. Upon seeing and hearing all that, the sailors thought they were going mad and jumped into the water. The moment they touched the water, they changed into dolphins, which were incapable of doing anyone any harm. From that moment on, they stood for kindness and virtue in the sea.

Plutarch
On the Cleverness of Animals
2nd century AD:

To the dolphin alone,
Beyond all others,
Nature has given what the best philosophers seek:
Friendship for no advantage. Though it has no need for man,
Yet it is the friend to all men and has often given them great aid.

Oppian's Halieutica (2nd century AD):

Diviner than the dolphins nothing is yet created; for indeed they were aforetime man and lived in cities along with mortals, but by the devising of Dionysos they exchanged the land for the sea and put on the form of fishes."

The first one to learn of their good nature was the god of the sea himself – Poseidon – or Neptune, as the Romans called him later:

Poseidon was looking for the dark-eyed Amphitrite to make her his bride. After searching for a long time, a dolphin succeeded in finding her and bringing her to Poseidon, since she had been hiding from him in a cavern in the sea. As a way of thanking the dolphin, Poseidon conferred the highest honor of all on the dolphin and placed it in the sky together with the rest of the constellations. In July, if you happen to be in the northern hemisphere, it can be seen hanging between Aquila and Pegasus.

One of Aesop's tales tells a beautiful story of a monkey and a dolphin. It has a moral, which teaches the wisdom of being quiet and modest. In my opinion, it also expresses admiration for the good-hearted dolphin that cannot tolerate foolishness and lying. It goes like this:

A ship was captured and men and animals that were no longer required were thrown into the sea. Among them was a monkey. It was swimming helplessly, trying to find a way out, when a dolphin, seeing its obvious distress, took the monkey on its back. They started to head toward the shore of Piraeus, the harbor of Athens, when the dolphin asked the monkey: "Are you an Athenian?" "Yes," answered the monkey, and added, "and from one of the best families." "Then you are probably familiar with Piraeus," said the dolphin. "Oh, of course, he is one of my best friends..." Upon hearing that, the dolphin, disgusted with the foolish monkey and with his pride, threw him into the water and swam away...

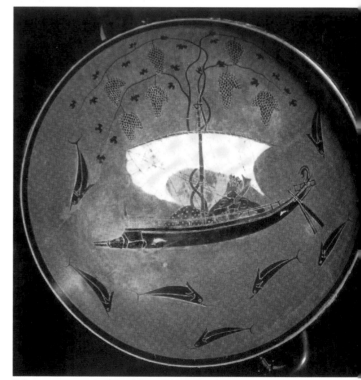

Dionysus cup, by Exekias. 540 BC.

In Mediterranean art and literature, there existed a vast body of myths and legends that was called "delphinology", which dealt with the strange and curious relationship between humans and dolphins. The ancient Greeks saw a direct link between dolphin and the deep and powerful strength of the water and the seas. Delphys, the Greek word for Dolphin, has an association with the word delphis, which actually means "womb". The theme of the dolphin as a transformed human is quite universal. It served as a tool for anthropomorphosis to explain the dolphin's intelligence and kindness to humans.

Dolphins mosaic from Volubilis, an ancient Roman ruins site in Marrocco. 3rd Century BC.

The dolphin rider at Iassos is a tale of love between a dolphin and a young boy. This legend is full of symbols – a powerful evocation of love and death, the destructive and creative elements of the sea, the beginning of the world and the dualistic nature of human sexuality. The tale has its roots in reality: that was a period of time in which fishermen had dolphins and whales as their close and frequent companions at sea (cooperating in fishing as well), and young boys and girls used to ride dolphins as part of their everyday lives. It was locally believed that killing a dolphin could unleash disastrous events in peoples' lives and as such was the worst possible omen. Here is the legend of the Dolphin of Iassos, written by Aelian (Roman author and teacher of Rhetoric, died 235 AD):

The Dolphin of Iassos

Iassos' gymnasium is near the sea
After running and wrestling all afternoon
The boys went down there and washed,
A custom from way back, when
One day a dolphin fell in love
With the loveliest boy of the time
At first when he paddled near the beach
The boy ran away in fear
But soon by staying close by and being kind
The dolphin taught the boy to love
They were inseparable
They played games
Swam side by side
Raced
Sometimes the boy would get up on top
And ride the dolphin like a horse
He was so proud his lover carried him around on his back
So were the town-people

Visitors were amazed
The dolphin used to take his sweetheart out to sea
Far as he liked
Then turn around
Back to the beach
Sat goodbye and return to the sea
The boy went home
When school was out
There would be the dolphin waiting
Which made the boy so happy
Everyone loved to look at him
He was so handsome
Men and women
Even (and that was the best part) the dumb animals
For he was the loveliest flower of boy ever was
But envy destroyed their love
One day the boy played too hard
Tired he threw himself down belly first
On the dolphin's back
Whose back spine happened to be pointing straight up

It stuck him in the navel
Veins split blood spilled
The boy died
The dolphin felt him riding heavier then usual
(the dead boy couldn't lighten himself by breathing)
Saw the sea turning purple from blood
Knowing what happened
He chose to throw himself on their beach by the gymnasium
Like a ship rushing through the waves
Carrying the boy's body? with him
They both lay there in the sand
One dead
The other gasping out life's breath
Iassos built them both a tomb
To requite their great love
They also set up a stele
Which shows a boy riding a dolphin
And put out silver and bronze coins
Stamped with the story of their love death
On the beach
They honor Eros the God who led boy and dolphin here

The image of a human riding on a dolphin must have enthralled the human psyche in many cultures around the world. For instance, riding a dolphin ensures a safe passage from birth to rebirth. It also has a more sexual, erotic meaning. The figure that encompasses both meanings above and beyond its importance in Roman mythology is Aphrodite. Images of Aphrodite riding a dolphin abound and indicate how deep the symbol penetrated human imagination. In one fascinating account of Aphrodite's birth, an egg fell into the water from the heavens. Fish gathered around it and saved it by bringing it to shore, where it was hatched by a dove to reveal Aphrodite. Archeological research in the Mycenean graves has uncovered ostrich eggs from the second millennium BC to which dolphin faïence was applied. The egg is interpreted the egg as a symbol of future life, and its surface represents the water over which dolphins convey the dead. At the same time, it is a symbol of the universe from which the goddess emerges after being carried to shore by dolphins. Vessels decorated with dolphin iconography were found in Minoan tombs, and were apparently used in rituals evoking the dolphin-womb association and symbolism. Interestingly enough, Eros, the male god, replaced Aphrodite in the role of the dolphin rider in Greek mythology in the seventh century BC, spawning a proliferation of dolphin images associated with the phallus, sky and wind. In Greek mythology, it would be Triton, the son of Poseidon (the Greek god of the sea) and Amphitrite, who was depicted as half dolphin, half man, holding a dolphin standing upright in his hand. Although the riders and the human figures changed, the dolphin remained a stable and profound symbol through various times and cultural phases.

Another ancient story comes from the town of Miletos, now in Turkey, but then a part of Greece. It was first told by Pylarchos and repeated long afterwards by Athenaios and Plutarch himself.

A man named Koiranos was a witness to some fishermen catching a dolphin in their net. He saw that they were about to kill it. He approached and begged then not to do that. He offered them some money and they were willing to release the dolphin back into the water. Some time later, he traveled on a ship with many other passengers and was shipwrecked off Mykonos, an island to the west. All the passengers on that ship drowned, while Koiranos was rescued – by a dolphin. When he died of old age in his native city many years later, his funeral was held near the seashore. While the body was burned, a group of dark dolphins appeared in the harbor, staying close to the shoreline. Witnesses said that it was just as if they were joining the funeral and mourning the death of their friend.

The Roman traveler Pliny the Elder (born 23 AD), who died when Vesuvius erupted in 79 AD, wrote a very famous work called Naturalis Historia. For the conclusion of his work, he was always on the lookout for interesting stories about animals, plants and nature in general. One of the most famous stories he heard was the following:

In the reign of Augustus, not far from the city of Naples, a dolphin fell tremendously in love with a certain young boy who used to go every noon to the Lucrine Lake. Now, at the time, the locals had a pet name for all dolphins: because of the shape of the dolphins' snouts, they called them Simo, which is a Greek word meaning "snubnose". Pliny says that the dolphins answered to that name and "liked it better than any other". Every day, attracting him with a piece of bread in his hand, he used to call it and wait for it impatiently. The dolphin would then appear, emerge from the water, take the bread and then offer his back to the boy to ride on. The boy would then ride the dolphin to Puteolli, where the boy's school was located. Then one day, after several joyful years, the boy became sick and died soon afterwards. The dolphin kept on coming to look for the boy, with a sorrowful air and manifesting every sign of deep affliction, until he finally died of pure sorrow and heartbreak.

Another story by the same author in Naturalis Historia recounts the following:

The dolphin is an animal that is not only very friendly to people, but a lover of music, and it is possible to charm and entertain it by singing to him in harmony. But it is the sound of the water organ that has the most impact on it. The dolphin is not afraid of human beings, as if they were something strange to it, but comes readily to meet passing vessels at sea and rides around them, as if trying to race with them.

Pliny also described what we know as the first known description of a dolphin escorting ships: "It is not afraid of human beings as something strange to it," he wrote, "but comes to meet vessels at sea and sports and gambols round them even when in full sail." He goes on to describe the dolphin as a social animal – a very accurate description for the first century AD: "The dolphins also have a form of public alliance of their own."

Oppian (second century AD) wrote the following beautiful description of dolphin strandings, perceiving them as the way dolphins choose to end their lives when they feel death is near:

This other excellent deed of dolphins have I heard and admired. When fell disease and fatal draws high to them, they fail not to know it but are aware of the end of life. Then they flee the sea and the wide waters of the deep and come aground on the shallow shores. And there they give up their breath and receive their doom upon the land; that so perchance some mortal man may take pity on the holy messenger of Poseidon when he lies low, and cover him with mound of shingle, remembering his gentle friendship; or do haply the seething sea herself may hide his body in the sands; nor do any of the brood of the sea behold the course of their lord, nor any foe do dishonor to his body even in death. Excellence and majesty attend them even when they perish, nor do they shame their glory even when they die...

Greek mythology tells us about the Apollo the sun god and how he defeated Delphyne, the dolphin/womb monster. As a result of his victory, he built a temple at Delphi and decided to take the title of Delphinius – "Dolphin-God". Then he became a giant dolphin and revealed himself as a god in Delphi. This is how Apollo emerged as a victorious god out of the sea of creation ready to command the whole universe.

Greek and Roman artists, inspired by stories of friendship between dolphins and human beings, combined dolphin images and motifs in mosaics and sculptures and even minted them on coins, since dolphins were believed to protect travelers. Coins with dolphins inscribed on them were placed in the palms of the dead to ensure them a safe journey to the afterworld. Around 650-500 BC, artists in Athens began to create beautiful pottery, uniquely decorated in black and red, depicting mythological scenes and figures.

Cretan artists of the Minoan civilization (1,400 BC to the fourth century BC) frequently used dolphin motifs in their works of art and decorative murals and frescoes. Their dolphins were unique in their realism, stylish sense of movement and colorful beauty. Recent archeological findings on the Greek island of Thera reveal a rich and dazzling source of dolphin iconography used in art and serves as yet another proof of the important status of dolphins in the Aegean culture. When we look at some of the frescos found, it seems clear that the artists reveled in nature, in the sea and, in particular, in dolphins, and celebrated this unique animal-man encounter with their vivid art. (see Cretan Dolphin fresco on page no. 169)

In Greek folklore from Zacynthos, Poseidon took a certain hero who fell into the sea and transformed him into a dolphin. The spell would last until the day he found a woman who would consent to be its wife. Some time later, the dolphin happened to save people from a sinking ship in which a king and his daughter were sailing. In order to express her gratitude, the princess asked the dolphin to be her husband. From that moment on, the spell was broken and he was transformed back into the hero.

Arion, the fifth-century poet and the most famous dolphin rider, wrote a hymn to Poseidon. There are several versions of the original, which was apparently lost. Here is one version:

Cretan dolphin fresco

Sea lord Poseidon
Golden trident
Biding earth in the child-swollen salt sea
You most high
Whom fish encircle
Dance about lightly
Fins up down
Back forward
Snub nose manes rippling
Running hard, sea pups
Dolphins music lovers
Briny kids
girl goddesses
Amphitrite's
Nereids
Milk-breast fed
Whose hump backs I rode
To Taenarum Cliffs
In Pelop's land

Furrowing the flat sea plains
A trackless way
The time the trickers
Threw me off their smooth ship
Into the swelling of salt purple sea.

Here is the story of Arion, a seventh-century BC poet and musician who was born on the Isle of Lesbos:

Arion used to travel across the country, singing and playing his lyre. One day, returning home from Sicily in his boat, a group of thugs robbed him and threatened to kill him. Arion asked them to grant him last wish: to be able to sing his last song. The robbers agreed. Arion sang and his poignant music traveled across the waves and suddenly, from all sides, dolphins appeared, encircling the boat. Arion leapt overboard right into the midst of the dolphins and one of them carried him straight to shore, with the whole group accompanying them. This is how Arion was saved.

As mentioned previously, the Greeks depicted dolphins in their works of art, on wall panels, on jars and vases and in many other crafts and ornaments. Here are some examples:

Oceanus: 1st- 2nd century AD

A bronze coin depicting the Titan, Oceanus. His bearded face emerges from the background. In keeping with artistic realism, Oceanus is portrayed as a bearded old man, not as a monster or an abstract force of nature. Locks of wavy hair frame his face and his eyes shine with silver, as do his cheeks, nose and forehead. Two dolphins leap from the top of his head, forming a sort of a crown and celebrating the ocean and its most important inhabitants with Oceanus as its ruler.

Native Americans

In the Tlingit American Indian myth, we learn of the origin of the Orca or killer whale.

A man by the name of Natsilane had constant arguments and quarrels with his own wife. His wife's brothers were always on his wife's side. Wishing to protect their sister, they took Natsilane one day and left him alone on a deserted island. Natsilane started to carve images of whales out of different kinds of bark and woods. Every time he finished with the creation of a whale, he took it to the water and let it sail. But the images simply floated for a while and then returned to him unchanged. He started to carve them out of yellow cedar. This time it was different: the images floated, started to swim like killer whales, changed into killer whales, swam far into the sea, came back to him and finally changed back into wooden images. He made holes in their dorsal fins and holding on to them, went with them to the sea. One day, he saw his brothers-in-law leaving the shore with their canoes and sailing into the sea. He put his images into the water. The whales smashed the canoes and killed his wife's brothers as if they were frail matchsticks. Natsilane told his whales' spirits: "From now on you are not to hurt any humans anymore. You must be kind to them."

Ecuador

A story from Ecuador tells us about an unfaithful wife and her lover who transform themselves into dolphins after being discovered by her husband.

Australia

The Aborigines of Australia take the theme of transformation as far as it can go: They believe that they are the direct descendents of dolphins. They perform rituals that involve dancing and chanting and induce a trance-like state. It is fascinating to learn that in this state, which is called "dream-time", the Aborigines reach a high plane where the ultimate goal is actually communicating with dolphins. Every time such a ritual is performed, they are reunited with the dolphins, and the bond that exists between them from ancient times is reaffirmed and strengthened.

Only until around 150 years ago in Moreton Bay on the Pacific coast of Queensland, the Aborigines used to catch mullet with the help of dolphins. According to various accounts, the Aborigines understood the dolphins and knew how to call them. They even had particular names for individual dolphins. They forbade the killing of dolphins and believed that dreadful consequences would follow if a dolphin were killed. The director of the Queensland Museum collected all the references made to this extraordinary cooperation and published it in a book called Memoirs. Here is a short extract from it:

For my part I cannot doubt that the understanding is real, and that the natives know these porpoises, and that strange porpoises would not show so little fear of the natives. The oldest men of the tribe say that the same kind of fishing has always been carried out for as long as they can remember. Porpoises abound in the bay, but in no other part do the natives fish with their assistance.

Jordan

It is a fascinating fact that due to the popular use of the dolphin as a symbol of good luck and, in particular, as an amulet for safe journeys, other faraway cultures that originally had no contact with dolphins were influenced and began to incorporate them into objects of art. An example of this is the Nabatean culture in Jordan. In the ruins of a Nabatean temple at Khirbet Tannur, a stone image of royalty was uncovered, wearing a crown of dolphins on her head. It now seems probable that the nomadic nature of the Nabatean way of life brought them to numerous Mediterranean seaports, where dolphin images were venerated in Hellenistic Europe, Africa and Asia.

Lord Byron, England

The poet, Lord Byron, refers to dolphins in his "Childe Harold's Pilgrimage". He describes the sad death of a dolphin:

Parting Day

Dies like the dolphin, whom each pang imbues
With a new color as it gasps away;
The last still loveliest, till 'tis gone, and
All is gray.

Brazil

The local fishermen of Brazil, who know the Amazon River so well, can tell many stories regarding the Amazon River dolphin, the Bouto. They believe that the Bouto is a creature that can change shape and assume human form. They also believe that it can rise up from the water and try to seduce young girls from the village by means of enchanting dances. A beautiful legend tells the story of a young girl and a dolphin:

Once upon a time, there was a very beautiful girl who used to go bathing in the river. She didn't know, but every time she was there, in the water, a dolphin would watch her from afar. The dolphin felt that from the first moment he set his eyes on her, he knew that all he wanted was to be with her. One day, the girl went to the river to wash before the great Full Moon ball in the village, which was a very exciting event for her. She went to the ball with her boyfriend, but the Bouto (believed to be able to assume human form) was actually the most handsome man there. The first time she looked at him, she fell in love immediately. They were so much in love that their senses almost ceased to function. Then, one of the men from the village guessed that this was actually a dolphin and not a real person and he chased the dolphin away. The next ball came, and the girl knew he would come. And he did. They danced happily all night and then went to the river. They lay there in the sand on the riverbank and made love, after which the dolphin suddenly leapt up and disappeared into the water. She was heartsick and, not knowing what to do, went to the local Shaman and asked him for help. The Shaman asked the Mother of the Lake to help. The Mother of the Lake asked the moon to help, since the girl, as they found out, was pregnant. The Shaman knew that the father was a dolphin.

At the next ball, when the moon was full, it asked the dolphin to come. The dolphin obeyed and joined his lover. The girl told him that she was carrying his child in her womb. Upon hearing that, the dolphin had to explain why he had left her so cruelly. "I love you and want to be with you, but I can only see you at the ball, since I can only assume the form of a human being on those nights." Many months had passed before the next ball - exactly nine, in fact. And then the girl brought the baby to

the Bouto of the Amazons

the boy so that he could see his son. And so it continued for all their lives, meeting at the balls, dancing together and then parting until the next one."

Many people in the village believe in this story and there are girls today who come to the festivities in the hope of meeting a Bouto.

Polynesia

The Maoris, a branch of the Polynesian people who later migrated to New Zealand, were great sea-dwellers and fish eaters. On their islands, they spent half of their lives in the water and became well acquainted with all the animals of the sea. The Maori name for a dolphin was aihe. They knew how to distinguish it from porpoises and whales, for which they had different names. Some anthropologists believe that the legendary creatures named taniwha that appear in their myths, tales and legends are actually dolphins, because the ocean taniwha are always benevolent, gentle and helpful.

Bora Bora
Tahaa
Huahine
Teriaroa
Raitea
Polynesia
Tahiti
Moorea

There is a story about a man who was punished by being trapped in the body of a porpoise forever. Another tells about a taniwha that came to the rescue of a small boy who was drowning in the sea. Maori tales tell of groups of taniwha that used to accompany boasts and ships and guide them to islands they could not find. The Maoris were always wise and knowledgeable enough to know how to call a dolphin in cases of need, using special invocations. One of the famous stories involving dolphins is the following:

Te Whare was a little boy, five years of age. He was the son of one of the chiefs of the Ngaphui tribe. The Ngaphui had planned to go on an expedition, probably for the purpose of raiding some other tribe. Te Whare and his father were in the leading boat, together with the commander, a young man. Because of a dispute between the younger commander and the boy's father, the young one decided, together with the others on board, to throw the little boy overboard. He said to the father:"Your son will be thrown into the sea and will quench the fire that is burning within you, me and the others." At his signal, strong hands grasped the fragile little boy and threw him over the side of the boat. The boy's father watched all this without showing any emotion at all. Silently, without showing the others what he was doing, he started to whisper certain invocations to call for the taniwha to help his son. From that moment on, he had placed his son's life in the hands of the dolphins. The canoe continued sailing and no one felt a thing. Secretly the father glanced back and he saw a dolphin approaching the canoe. In those times, a taniwha

made its presence felt by bumping the boat underneath to let the voyagers know that they were safe, no matter what happened in the sea. Only the father felt the gentle touch of the dolphin from underneath the canoe. Then, the taniwha swam to the boy. Te Whare was terrified – he thought that a great monster had come to eat him, but the taniwha, understanding the boy's fear, played around him and finally, when the boy was exhausted, carried him on his back and took him to the nearest point of land. He left him there and disappeared. Some women from the village found Te Whare and brought him to their home. Unfortunately, they decided to keep him as a slave and worse still, in a tribe that was hostile to his own. He grew into an incredible man with special powers and became a chief among his own people, following in his father's footsteps.

Dolphin Reef, Eilat, Israel
Website: www.dolphinreef.co.il

Chapter 12

Dolphins in modern myths and literature

The important role dolphins have always played in global literature, art and myths is certainly amazing. Even more tantalizing, however, is the fact that people are still creating myths about them. In fact, dolphins seem to have evolved into animals of extraordinary powers and senses in the human psyche, animals endowed with inexplicable qualities such as their friendliness toward humans and the way they seem to seek human company and contact.

Many modern books and films revolve around dolphins. The movie, Free Willy, made a huge impact on people. While it contributed to people's awareness of dolphins in captivity, it also greatly enhanced the creation of myths regarding dolphins and whales.

Modern myths are sometimes enhanced through mystical and mental concepts of dolphins that are brought upon by apparently "authorized: figures. See chapter on Therapy for further details (i.e., works of a Psychologist who believes dolphins can heal from afar and others).

Modern-day writers and authors have written novels in which dolphins are either the main characters or are introduced into the novels in different ways.

Douglass Adams, who wrote the best-selling trilogy about a futuristic world (The Hitchhiker's Guide to the Galaxy / The Restaurant at the End of the World / So Long and Thanks for All the Fish (Wing Books 1994), mentions dolphins in Chapter 23 of The Hitchhiker's Guide to the Galaxy in the following brilliant way:

"It is an important and popular fact that things are not always what they seem: For instance, on planet Earth Man has always assumed that he was more intelligent than Dolphins because he had achieved so much – the wheel, New York and wars and so on – while all the dolphins had ever done was muck about

in the water having a good time. But conversely, the dolphins had always believed that they were far more intelligent than man – for precisely the same reasons.

Curiously enough, the dolphins had long known of the impending destruction of the planet Earth and had made many attempts to alert mankind to the danger, but most of their communications were misinterpreted as amusing attempts to punch footballs and whistle for tidbits, so they eventually gave up and left the Earth by their own means shortly before the Vogons arrived.

The last-ever message was misinterpreted as a surprisingly sophisticated attempt to do a double-backward somersault through a loop while whistling the "Star Spangled Banner", but in fact the message was this: So long and thanks for all the fish."

In 1969, Robert Merle wrote a novel called The Day of the Dolphin (New York: Simon and Schuster; London: Weidenfeld & Nicolson), which is a drama about a brilliant scientist who, while involved in important research, tries to communicate with another species – dolphins – for the first time. It is about humans and dolphins caught up in man's mindless and violent race toward his own extinction. When the novel was published, some people claimed that it was in fact a novel based on Dr. John Lilly's work on dolphins (see Chapter 10 for further details), but the author dismissed these suggestions.

In 1973, David Mason wrote a novel called The Deep Gods (New York: Lancer) about a planet on which man and dolphin communicated and were linked by a common bond – The Great Compact of Life. When dolphins sang their hypnotic music, the sea and all its creatures went into an ecstatic celebration. The protagonist, Daniel, had to save the power that holds all life together.

A novel called The Dolphin and the Deep was written by Thomas Burnett Swann and was first published by Nova Publications in 1963. It is about an explorer who is accompanied by other humans and a female white dolphin in his life's quests. The dolphins are portrayed as highly intelligent, playful and noble beings, who expect to be acknowledged for their service to man. They also bring good luck into people's lives.

Arthur C. Clarke, one of the most famous science fiction writers, wrote a novel called Dolphin Island (Berkeley Publishing Co.: 1963). In it we learn of a young stowaway who is rescued by "the people of the sea" and who in turn helps them defeat an enemy even more ancient and ruthless than man.

In 1981, Tristan Jones wrote a novel called Aka (Macmillan Publishing) about Conan, a middle-aged adventurer who has entered a boat race, during the course of which he falls overboard into the water. In a wonderful tale, the dolphin Aka and other dolphins relate to Conan, communicate with him and keep him afloat. The dolphins depicted in the story are bottlenose dolphins, and the reader learns about their lives as well as Conan's own story.

The Blue Dolphin by Robert Barnes (Tiburon, California: 1992) is a novel about a dolphin that feels the need to live his life apart from its community. Propelled by its curiosity and independent spirit, it leaves and becomes a lone dolphin that interacts with humans out of its own free will.

Brotherhood of Dolphins by Ricardo Means Ybarra (Arte Publico Press: 1997) is the story of a detective who is searching for a certain criminal. The search takes him back to his youth. The psycho protagonist, Billy Johnson, is a dolphin lover who espouses a New Age philosophy related to pyramids, dolphins and swimming with them and the whole new tendency to return to nature. In his mind, his philosophy justifies murder and arson.

Children of the Sea by Wilfred S. Bronson was written in 1940 (Harcourt, Brace and Co.). It tells the story of young boy who helps a wounded dolphin recover; the two become friends in the process. Although published as early as 1940, the book is full of details about dolphins' intelligence, friendliness and biologically accurate facts. Today it is a rare book, since it is out of print.

In 1981, Steve Senn wrote a novel called A Circle in the Sea. It is about Bree, a quiet, dreamy, young female dolphin that is troubled by dreams about the Others – namely, human beings. The other character, a girl who lives in Florida, is having strange dreams as well. In fact, her mind inhabits the body of a dolphin – to be precise, a dolphin named Bree. Through these experiences she learns how dolphins live, communicate and think, and she also meets many dolphins in her supernatural world.

The Dolphins of Altair by Margaret St. Clair (Dell: 1967), is a novel about the covenant between the land and the sea people that existed before the dawn of man. Only certain creatures – the dolphins – remembered this covenant. The people who remained on shore forgot all about it.

In 1994, Anne McCaffrey wrote a novel called The Dolphin of Pern (Ballantine Books), which revolves around the first humans who came to settle the planet Pern. They did not come alone: intelligence-enhanced dolphins crossed the stars to colonize the oceans of the new planet. Then a mysterious disaster befell them and the people's hopes and dreams were shattered. The dolphins were forgotten with time, but the dolphins themselves never forgot and continued to transmit their history on from generation to generation in the hope of preserving the memory of their past friends. Then, as a response to a new threat, the dolphins and people reconnect and the bond between them is revived.

In 1981, Ted Mooney wrote a novel called Easy Travel to Other Planets (Vintage Books). It is a story about a unique relationship that develops between a woman and a dolphin, who live together in a house that has a flooded floor (just like the one Dr. Lilly had in his laboratory and which was built for the purpose of studying dolphin communication and life). The woman has to deal with a new kind of love in her life – the love of a dolphin.

Jim Cummings wrote a book called A Friend in the Water: Tales of Sea and Sky, (Healing Earth Publications: 1988) about the spiritual connection between dolphins and humans and tells the story of a young boy and his experiences with a dolphin.

Island of the Blue Dolphins is a very famous book written by Scott O'Dell in 1968 (Dell Publishing) and published again years later. The story is based on some true facts: In 1835, an Indian tribe was evacuated from an island off the coast of California and two small children were left behind. Eighteen years later, a woman who spoke no recognizable language was found with her dog. She was unable to communicate except through sign language. On the basis of this, Scott wrote a moving novel about her solitary existence.

King of the Sea, by Derek Bickerton (Random House: 1979) is a story about Andy Holliday who becomes one with the species he is trying to save, and in this different world, not so far away from ours, he finds loyalty, love and humanity.

Song of the Dolphins: A South Seas Mystical Adventure by Derek Ryan, is a novel about the journey of two bottlenose dolphins, Odin and Mira, and their discovery of secret teachings of the great whale masters.

Star Seed by David Andreissen (The Donning Co.: 1982) is a novel about a few humans and dolphins that are the only survivors of a terrible epidemic that wipes out the entire planet. They all live in an underground laboratory with no exposure to air. They set out in a small submarine to find the cause of the cause of the plague.

Chapter 13

New Age spirituality and dolphins

As we have seen, dolphins have been part of an extensive body of myth, literature and art through the ages and in many different cultures around the world. However, if we look at the important place dolphins hold in people's minds and psyches today, we realize that dolphins have never lost their power over the human mind. Indeed, myths about dolphins' ability to help humans is not a thing of the past. A large group of people around the world (of different spiritual inclinations) attribute spiritual and esoteric characteristics to dolphins and aspire to spend time with them in order to learn from them, be healed through them or grow spiritually through their wise guidance. Groups of people travel long distances in order to swim with dolphins; pregnant women want to swim with them so that the dolphins, feeling the embryo, will contribute to its development and health; other pregnant women seek to give birth in the water, surrounded by dolphins, and so on.

When it comes to dolphins, we find that New Age concepts of spirituality are born not only from spiritual groups, but also from scientific sources. One example that made an impact on the way people think about dolphins is the work of Dr. John Lilly (1915-2001), founder of the organization called Cetacean Nation (see Appendix for further details).

The organization calls for a new way of thinking as we recognize that another intelligent and conscious species that occupies the waters of the earth has evolved around us.

It states: "Not only do cetaceans represent a decided shift in human intelligence by accepting another sentient race on the planet, but with this new association, may also be considered to be emotional balancing and healing agents for the troubled hearts of mankind. Add to this the understanding that dolphins and whales represent a spiritual manifestation on this physical plane and it moves to establish an even higher consciousness connection for all to observe and become a participant. Open up your minds and hearts to this new sensation and way of being. Feel the joy and peace of the Fifth Dimensional Awareness – Pod Mind Mentality. It awaits your acceptance and realization. We are no longer alone in the universe. We are awaking to who we really are: Lightbeings connected to the Source of All that IS. The cetaceans have anticipated this moment for three thousand years, inviting us to rejoin them in this joyful recognition and new understanding of this liberated state of being."

Appendix

The Cetacean Nation

The Cetacean Nation was a product of the incredible mind of Dr. John Lilly, who was one of the most original thinker in modern research in general and the study of dolphins in particular (see Chapter 10 for further details). Dr. John Lilly died in 2001 at age 86. The following extract was taken from the Cetacean Nation website (www.cetacean-nation.com) and outlines the principles of the organization, its ideals, beliefs and call for action.

"Just as any group of people in the human society has learned to identify itself and has developed adequate spokesmen for its causes, so it is the right of all cetaceans, dolphins and whales, to have someone to speak for them. Recognized as having brains which are in some ways even more biologically complex than humans, and having complex social structures, language and behavior, the question remains: should cetaceans be given individual rights under the human laws?

The future of many species of whales and dolphins is in question. The Baiji, or the Yangtze River dolphin, the Vaquita dolphins found in the sea of Cortez, and the North Pacific whales are but a few species whose chance of being completely exterminated from our earth during the next two decades is almost a certainty.

From the Cetacean Nation website:

As each group of humans, through its own experience, learned to feel its lack of sharing in the benefits of laws and their administration, each developed adequate spokesmen or spokeswomen for its cause. These individuals were either inside or outside the group needing relief.

This same situation can now be seen reflected in the existence of cetaceans. Recognized as having brains which are in some ways even more biologically complex than humans, and having complex social structures, languages and socials behaviors which are also at least as complex as humans, the question remains: should cetaceans be given individual rights under human laws?

The size and complexity of the cetacean brain has been known for many years. Only recently has microscopic analysis shown that their cellular densities and connections are quite as large and complex as our own.

Throughout history, through to the present day, human beings have conducted large-scale acts of genocide upon each other. Even today, in many parts of the world, we can observe the mass slaughter of our own species. BosniaHercegovina, Somalia and Cambodia are but a few examples of this. At the same time, a similar mass-annihilation of highly evolved intelligent and sentient creatures, the whales and dolphins, can also be seen throughout our world.

The future of many species of whales and dolphins is in question. The Baiji, or Yangtze River Dolphin, the Vaquita dolphin found in the Sea of Cortez, and the North Pacific Right Whale are but a few species whose chances of being completely exterminated from our earth during the next two decades is almost a certainty.

To insure the survival of cetaceans, in light of the continuous onslaught by their terrestrial counterparts, human beings, it is essential that cetaceans be recognized for what they truly are: non-terrestrial intelligent lifeforms. Lifeforms which do indeed have the same inherent rights that human beings have to survive and to live in peace.

The purposes of a Cetacean Nation are:

1) To foster greater understandings of the minds and consciousness of whales and dolphins;

2) To develop methods and technologies to enhance interspecies communications between humans and cetaceans

3) To gain recognition from the international human community to the inherent rights that cetaceans have, which include:

- Freedom from mass specicide by human hands
- Freedom to live in their aquatic world and nurture their young
- Freedom to echo their own thoughts on their futures

The Cetacean Nation has long-term plans that include political and legal rights for whales and dolphins, formation of a communication center and databank, an information center and center for the development of communication means between human and cetaceans."

glossary

Aerial behavior – Forms of dolphin and whale behavior that involves leaps, jumps, and bow riding, among other things, all of which occur above the surface of the water and can thus be observed from afar. It is an important tool in dolphin research, since these actions are all external manifestations of dolphins' communicative and/or playful behavior.

Altruism – Helping behavior in which an individual performs a costly behavior for the welfare of another individual/whole group.

Blowhole – A special hole located on top of the dolphin's head through which air is inhaled and exhaled. As opposed to other mammals whose nostrils are located in the anterior part of their head, in dolphins and whales the blowhole is found on top of the head in order to prevent the penetration of water into the lungs.

Bow riding – The action of riding or surfing the ocean waves. It seems that this is one of the things dolphins enjoy most. Sometimes a whole school of dolphins can be seen surfing the waves, and it is one of the most beautiful dolphin-related sights we can witness.

Cetacean – A dolphin, a whale, or a porpoise.

Delphinidea – A taxonomic family that includes many species of dolphins.

Echolocation – A unique sense that enables the dolphins to detect and hunt individual prey. Ultrasonic sound is produced in the melon – a structure located on top of the dolphin's head – and is emitted in the form of a beam. Sound waves that return to the inner ear provide the dolphin with information regarding its surroundings and prey.

Mysticetes– A taxonomic suborder that diverged from Odontocetes (see entry) along the evolutionary tree, to include Right whales, the gray whale and rorquals. They filter-feed on large shoals of prey that comprises mainly phytoplankton, and do not possess the sense of echolocation.

Odontocetes – A taxonomic suborder of toothed whales; this suborder includes sperm whales, white whales, porpoises, dolphins, and river dolphins. They have teeth, as opposed to the Mystecetes (see entry), and they use echolocation to hunt individual prey.

River dolphins – A group of dolphins that live in the major rivers of the world, including the Amazon in Brazil, the Ganges in India, the Yangtze in China, and the Irrawady in Myanmar, to name a few. These dolphins are relatively unknown because of their shyness, small numbers, and geographical locations, and it is only in recent years that worldwide attention has focused on their situation. It is regrettable to note that their populations are declining due to the hunting, destruction, and pollution that characterize their habitats.

S-curve position – When courting a female, the male bottlenose dolphin bends its body into a S-curve shape, with its tail and head up, in front of her.

Signature whistle – A personal whistle that serves as the dolphin's "fingerprint", enabling the other members of the group to identify each and every individual. It is a crucial component in the contact between the mother and her baby.

Spy hopping – A form of cetacean (see entry) behavior that consists of rising vertically out of the water, head first, and scanning the entire surrounding area while rotating.

Strandings – Whales or dolphins that are found stranded on beaches. There are two types of strandings: in the first, corpses of whales and dolphins are found on the seashore; in the second, live whales and dolphins drift ashore. This phenomenon is still not well understood, and many theories have been advanced to explain it.

Tail slapping – Also called lobtailing. Dolphins can be seen slapping their tails forcibly on the surface of the water. This might be a sign of anger or a manifestation of aggressive behavior, and as such is an important form of external behavior used in dolphins' communication.

Author Galia Dor with a friend. Dolphin Reef, Eilat, Israel.